D1171249

THE BOOK OF
MULES

THE
BOOK
OF
MULES:

SELECTING,

BREEDING,

AND

CARING

FOR

EQUINE

HYBRIDS

DONNA CAMPBELL SMITH

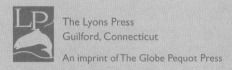

The Lyons Press
Guilford, Connecticut
An imprint of The Globe Pequot Press

The Lyons Press is an imprint of The Globe Pequot Press.

Design by Sheryl P. Kober
Layout by Melissa Evarts
Unless otherwise noted, all photos are courtesy of the author.

Library of Congress Cataloging-in-Publication Data

Campbell, Donna, 1946-
 The book of mules : selecting, breeding, and caring for equine hybrids / Donna Campbell Smith.
   p. cm.
 Includes bibliographical references and index.
 ISBN 978-1-59921-283-8 (alk. paper)
1. Mules I. Title.
SF362.C36 2008
636.1'83—dc22   2008024538

Printed in China

10 9 8 7 6 5 4 3 2 1

Contents

Waiting patiently.

Preface

Uncle Corey wasn't actually an uncle but the husband of a distant cousin on my mother's side. It's a Southern thing. They lived on a little farm on Backwoods Road in Roper, North Carolina. Uncle Corey had a mule that inspired my imagination whenever we visited. I wanted to ride that mule because in my mind it was a horse. I'd wanted a horse since I could remember. I pretended to be a cowgirl, or sometimes an Indian, riding across vast open lands at full gallop on my imaginary horse. So the prospect of riding a real one seemed like a wonderful dream come true.

One day I was tagging after Daddy and Uncle Corey out by the barn, leaving Mama and my sister inside doing the dishes with Aunt Franny. Uncle Corey also had a whiskey still, and my guess, now I am grown up, is they were having an after-dinner drink. That might also be why they relented to my pleas to ride the mule. Uncle Corey put a halter on the big, brown creature, and Daddy lifted me up onto its bare, bony back. I was terrified, and that was just while we were standing still. Fear of falling, one of the primal fears, I have read, intensified as soon as my cousin-by-marriage-uncle began to lead the mule off at a walk. When I started to cry, Daddy picked me off the mule's back and sent me back to the house. That was the last time I asked to ride Uncle Corey's mule.

I remember one other mule from my childhood. This mule came to town on Saturday mornings, driven by an elderly black man who sold vegetables out of the cart. Down our street they came, the old man shouting out in a singsong rhythm the names of the vegetables and their prices. Sometimes it was fresh corn or green beans and butterbeans. We had a garden, so Mama didn't join the other ladies who came out of their houses to buy from the vegetable man.

But the neighborhood children and I would run out to meet and pet the mule, and we followed the vegetable man and his mule until they turned the corner and ambled off to another street, the vegetable man calling out, "Watermelons! Watermelons! Fifty cents; get your watermelons!"

History moved on and the vegetable man and his mule stopped coming to town. I never again heard the clip-clop of hooves on the paved road or the singsong of the driver's rich voice calling out his wares. Therefore, it is with a sense of recapturing the past I have written *The Book of Mules: Selecting, Breeding, and Caring for Equine Hybrids*. I have met some nice folks and their mules while gathering this information, and I believe it is a very good thing that mules have found their way back into our hearts. Look around you. They are out there still, serving in the military, carrying tourists into the Grand Canyon, and entertaining us under the spotlight. They are good companions that carry riders safely on the trail or to the winner's circle in the show ring and the racetrack. Mules are making a comeback.

Acknowledgments

I've always known horse people to be good folk. Now I know the same is true of mule people. I've met some great mule owners while writing this book. I thank them for sharing their knowledge and stories, for letting me photograph their mules, and for offering me their hospitality.

Shannon Hoffman asked me if I knew anything about mules when I first contacted her. She is owner of three mules, serves on the board of directors of the Carolina Mule Association, and is an active member of the North Carolina Horse Council. I felt a little intimidated. "Not really," I was forced to admit. Shannon fixed that by answering all my questions and letting me take her entire mule library home with me to help in my research. She introduced me to Seven, Sadie Mae, Shiloh, and Chester, the three mules and one donkey who share her life, and she provided contact information for other mule owners and experts. I spent three days at her farm photographing her mules, and she acted like she had all the time in the world, when the truth is she's a very busy lady. Thank you, Shannon.

Rocky, the trick mule, and James gave freely of their time and knowledge, too. I made at least three trips to photograph Rocky doing his amazing tricks. James and Rocky entertained my little group of riding students on a hot summer day, which had nothing to do with writing this book. I appreciate that. The kids had a ball. James replied to countless e-mails and phone calls

Rocky, the class clown.

with answers to my questions. Rocky, America's Ultimate Horse (Mule) Idol, and James, you rock!

I thank all the folks who answered questions, shared their stories, and either allowed me to photograph their mules or provided pictures for my book. I am afraid to name names because I know I'll leave someone out. I couldn't have done it without you, and I thank you.

Rita Rosenkranz, thank you again for so expertly taking care of the business end of things. You are the epitome of what a good agent should be. Steven D. Price, thank you for sticking with me and for your expert editing and advice. You have helped me grow. Thank you, Lyons Press for giving me a third book.

Dear family and friends, how do you stand it? Thanks for your support and for listening. Dineane, Julia, Deborah, Jessica, Michael, and Camille, I love you.

CHAPTER ONE

The Origin and History of the Mule

Origin

Ancient documents tell us mules have been around for at least 3,000 years. Because the two species lived in close proximity, it is even possible that a crossing of a donkey and horse resulting in a mule foal may have occurred in nature. Records show mules were used in ancient Asia Minor as pack animals and laborers, turning the millstone to grind grain into meal, and for transportation. In Ancient Egypt, mules were a novelty; donkeys were used for general work, while horses were for racing and royal ceremonial occasions. The Greek and Romans valued the mule for its strength and stamina. Because ancient Greeks used mules as well as horses in chariot races, the mule was also valued for its speed. In these races two mules were hooked to a cart. The lineup of teams raced twelve laps around the stadium to determine the winner.

In Greek legend King Midas of Phrygia is often portrayed in art with the ears of a mule or a donkey; some believe this was a punishment from the god Apollo, while others believe it was a sign of his royal status. The mule is also mentioned in *The Iliad of Homer* in a passage depicting Hector's funeral:

> *Waked with the word the trembling sire arose,*
> *And raised his friend: the god before him goes:*
> *He joins the mules, directs them with his hand,*
> *And moves in silence through the hostile land.*

Mules are mentioned several times in the Old Testament of the Bible. In 2 Samuel 13:29, when King David's son Absalom takes revenge and plans the murder of his brother Amnon, who had raped his sister, the rest of King David's sons fled on their mules. In 1 Kings 1:33 and 38, King David ordered that his son Solomon be given his own royal mule to ride when Solomon was to be anointed as the future king of Israel. In 1 Chronicles 12:40, mules were among the gifts the people of the tribes of Israel brought to David as tribute when he became the king.

Middle Ages

During the Middle Ages, while the great horse was used for heavy work like carrying knights and their massive armor, mule trains were the most common mode of transporting goods across country. Roads, when they existed at all, were too rough in many places for wagons. Long trains of a hundred or more mules led by their muleteers carried burdens of two hundred up to four hundred pounds. The mule trains were easy targets for land pirates and enemies, so knights rode along with the trains to protect them. In fact, the mule train was used in Spain until the twentieth century for commercial and military transport.

Peter the Hermit, a zealous prophet of the first century, rode a mule through France to proclaim his doctrines and call to arms Christian Europe for the salvation of Jerusalem from Muslim rule, thus instigating the First Crusade. People became so enraptured by Peter that they clamored to touch him and even took hairs from his mule as holy relics. Thus, Peter the Hermit's mule may well have been the first, and perhaps last, holy mule.

Ladies of the Middle Ages were partial to finely bred mules for general riding. Some were gaited and, along with fine horses, were called palfreys. Mules of that day were small compared to today's specimens.

When Columbus negotiated with King Ferdinand and Queen Isabella for funding to make his famous voyage, he rode to court on a mule provided by the Queen as part of the travel expenses. He was denied funding by Ferdinand, and Columbus left on the mule. But the Queen was not of the same mind as her husband, and she changed his mind. Isabella sent a messenger after Columbus, and when he turned the mule around and rode back to court, he was granted funds for the voyage. The rest is history.

Centuries later, navigating the Alps in snow and ice, Napoleon Bonaparte rode a mule borrowed from a Swiss peasant, not the rearing stallion he is pictured riding in artists' paintings. Napoleon did not go down in history as a gifted rider, so the mule was a better choice in terrain where sure-footedness and care were necessary. Napoleon won the campaign to take control of Austria from Italy when he crossed the Alps through the Great Saint Bernard Pass, using the element of surprise to defeat the Austrians in the Battle of Marengo. We can only wonder how things would have turned out had Napoleon not been riding a mule.

Mules in the New World

George Washington is generally credited with bringing the mule to America, or at least improving mule stock in this country. Mules were rare and expensive and, for the most part, mules raised in the colonies were exported back to the mother country. Washington's breeding program was aimed at producing a larger and stronger mule to be used on the farm. He imported donkeys from Spain, the first being a gift from King Charles III.

On October 26, 1785, Washington recorded that the first jack, appropriately named Royal Gift, arrived at Mount Vernon. Royal Gift was a shy breeder that first year, not being accustomed to mares. But he caught on by the following breeding season.

George Washington also received two jennets and a smaller jack from the Marquis de Lafayette. The jack, named The King of Malta, began a line of unsurpassed saddle mules. These mules from Washington's stock became the forerunners of quality mules that were the backbone of American agriculture for many generations of farmers.

Mules of early America were not only working on the farm, but they also pulled wagons and trolley cars in cities, hauled in the forests for the lumber industry, helped build railroads, and pulled barges along canals.

The C&O (Chesapeake and Ohio) Canal and many other canal systems used mules that were led along towpaths, often by children, to pull barges along their routes. The mules were stabled on the barge, living with the family that owned the barge, when they were not working. The average weight of barge mules was 1,000 pounds, and they stood about 15 hands tall. The mules proved better suited to the work than horses because they were sure-footed and hardy, and their tougher hides resisted harness sores as well. They were also cheaper than horses, averaging $125.

Posing in a tobacco field. Mules were the backbone of American agriculture for many generations of farmers.

Mules were used to pull gravity-powered trains up hills in mining regions and to pull street rail cars in cities. James Parker, originally a Cincinnati, Ohio, apple farmer, converted his orchards into an amusement park adding a dining hall, dance hall, and a mule-powered carousel. In 1886, he sold the park and it was called Ohio Grove; later it became known as the Coney Island of the West. The mule-turned merry-go-round was just the first of many rides and carnival games. It continued operation as a park until the 1960s.

Westward Movement

The mule proved to be invaluable to those who explored and settled the West. Mules were able to subsist on less food than oxen or horses and proved to be more sure-footed and agile in the mountainous terrain. In his book *The Mule Alternative: The Saddle Mule in the American West*, Mike Stamm cites testimony from the journals of explorers, soldiers, settlers, and gold rushers, who wrote of the mule's superior attributes over other beasts used for transportation.

While oxen may have been stronger and could pull a heavier load than a mule or horse, they were slow and could not manage on the meager grazing and water available when crossing deserts. Horses were perhaps faster than the mule but lacked their stamina and fell by the wayside when food and water were scarce. Many of the diary excerpts in Stamm's book tell of a mule carrying on to the end of the journey while horses and oxen died of starvation or had to be shot to put them out of their misery. One reason mules survived was that they ate almost anything when normal forage was not available. Zenas Leonard left St. Louis with an expedition of mountain men to trap and trade with Indians in the Rocky Mountains. By winter they were left with just two mules, all the horses having starved to death. Leonard wrote of the mules' diet in his diary: "The snow was still deep on the top of it [the mountain]; but by aid of the buffalo trails, we were enabled to scale it without much difficulty, except that our mules suffered with hunger, having had nothing to eat but pine brush. At the foot of the mountain we found abundance of sweet cottonwood, and our mules being very fond of it, we detained two or three days to let them recruit from their suffering in crossing the mountains." The expedition went ahead to Santa Fe to buy more horses and mules, leaving the surviving mules behind with four men to guard them and the furs and supplies until their return.

The personality of the mule was not so bragged about but rather was reported as vexing. Ernest Ingersol, a journalist reporting from the Hayden Scientific Expeditions of the 1870s, wrote, "It is my honest opinion, founded upon much observation, that so long as any considerable numbers of mules are employed there, it is utterly useless for missionaries to go to the Rocky Mountains."

But it was the mule's ability to jump from one rocky outcropping to another and negotiate those Rocky Mountains safely that made the westward movement a success.

The San Antonio to San Diego Mail Line:
The Jackass Mail

Until the conception of the San Antonio–San Diego (SAAD) Mail Line, military couriers took mail from the East to the West whenever it was convenient. James E. Birch, a businessman from Rhode Island, won the contract for the SAAD from the U.S. government in 1857. Birch had moved west and became president of The California Company, the largest stagecoach company in the world.

The first run left San Antonio July 9, 1857. Fifty-three days later James E. Mason and Samuel Ames rode in on mules ahead of the mail wagon, going down in history as the first to complete the run.

That first run used six armed men, one wagon, and nineteen mules. Another coach and twenty-seven mules were sent ahead for relay. Indians attacked them and stole all the mules. After that first run, the mail met the established standard of over 1,475 miles in thirty days each time, without fail. On the third run, three coaches made the trip with seventeen armed men, thirty-eight mules, and 4,000 pounds of rations and supplies.

The company worked hard to take good care of the mules. The mules were unhitched and allowed to graze at midday when the train stopped for dinner. After the meal break, a fresh team was hitched to the coach for the remainder of the day. The extra mules followed along unrestrained, as they had been trained to do. At night an armed guard was assigned to watch the mules in case of Indian raids.

The trail dipped down into Mexico after leaving San Antonio, then headed northwest back into the United States at Monument Station. At the James Lassiter Station, the people rested and had a good meal. From there they left the coaches behind and rode muleback from Mason Valley up to Oriflamme Canyon to the rim, after which they picked up another coach to San Diego.

Owner James E. Birch drowned in September 1857, a passenger on a ship that sank off Cape Hatteras, North Carolina. The mail line contract was then awarded to John Butterfield, owner of The Butterfield Overland Stage Company. They ceased running in 1861 after the beginning of the Civil War, because the southern route to the St. Louis terminal was no longer safe. The next company to run the mail was Wells Fargo.

Over six hundred mules, most from Missouri breeders, were used in the Jackass Mail Line, not donkeys, as the nickname would suggest. Civic leaders in the San Francisco and Sacramento areas wanted the contract and the mail line to come to their cities. Showing their disappointment when they did not win the contract, newspapers in those cities called it The Jackass Mail as a slur, or perhaps they did not know the difference between a mule and a donkey.

Borax Twenty Mule Teams

The Pacific Coast Borax Company was founded in the late 1800s. Borax, called the "miracle mineral" in those days, was used for everything from medicines to washing carriages. Today it is an ingredient in cleaning products and cosmetics and is used in the production of glass, ceramics, and agricultural products.

In 1881 William T. Coleman filed a claim to hundreds of acres of borax in Death Valley. Although the ore was right on the surface of the ground, Coleman had to find a way to transport it out of the valley to his customers by way of the Mojave railroad station.

He and his superintendent hired a muleskinner named Ed Stiles. Stiles came up with the idea of combining two ten-mule teams into one twenty-mule hitch. The one-hundred-foot-long team would pull two wagons and a water tank. The total weight was over thirty-six tons. The route was a grueling 165 miles across rugged mountains, plus a 50-mile trek across the desert. In summer the temperature sometimes reached 130° F.

The team had to be specially trained for this feat, with each mule having a specific job. The two mules in the front were the lead mules. The next ten were called the swing team. They were required to respond to the commands "stop" and "pull." Behind the swing team were three pairs of mules called the pointers, sixes, and eights. Whenever the team had to turn a sharp corner, these pairs were trained to jump over the eighty-foot-long chain that connected the whole team. The mules jumped the chain and pulled at an angle away from the curve to keep the chain going around the curve. The last pair, located just in front of the wagon, was called the wheelers. They were the largest and strongest members of the team and were often draft horses.

The Borax Twenty Mule Team was truly remarkable, but railroads and new borax fields made their job obsolete after five years of service. They continued to do exhibitions into the turn of the twentieth century, including the World's Fair in 1904 and various parades. In 1940 a movie was made about them, and they traveled from city to city to promote *Twenty Mule Team*. Pacific Coast Borax Company was one of the sponsors for *Death Valley Days*, a television series of stories about the Old West that ran from 1952 through 1975. A host introduced the programs; one of the hosts was Ronald Reagan.

The Pacific Coast Borax Company registered The Twenty Mule Team as their trademark in 1894. The team was reformed in the 1980s and continues to perform for special occasions.

One of the most amazing things about the famous Borax Twenty-Mule Teams is that over a five-year period of hauling more than twenty million pounds of borax out of Death Valley 165 miles to Mojave, not one mule was lost. This record can also be attributed to the mule's uncanny ability to take care of itself in the harshest conditions.

Mule Racing

On Southern plantations after the work was done, mules were used for racing. What began as a lark on the farm soon developed into a highly competitive pastime. Soon plantation owners, using slaves as jockeys, were fiercely competing with each other; of course, a good wager was involved. As competition continued, some owners kept mules that were used only for racing. Racing moved from the plantation to county fairs, and mule racing was often included at horse racing tracks. In 1895 mule racing was held at the Johnson County Fair in Kansas.

By the twentieth century, mule racing was a major sport held on race-tracks throughout the country, but mainly in the Deep South. Karen Glynn writes in her article "Running Mules: Mule Racing in the Mississippi Delta" that mule racing, complete with pari-mutuel betting, took place in several towns. Betting on horse racing was illegal in Mississippi, but they got around the law since it didn't "say anything about mules."

Mule racing was also enjoyed "up north." Long Island, New York, held mule races on the Newmarket track, America's first racecourse, circa 1668. The

Huckleberry Frolic was held annually at Newmarket and included mule races on its program, along with many other festivities.

In the fall of 1921, it was reported in the *New York Times* that Mrs. Theodore Roosevelt Jr. and Mrs. J. Griswold Webb would participate in a mule race at the Dutchess County Fair. Whether the ladies were to actually ride the mules themselves or they were merely the mule owners, the article did not say. Two Mississippi locations where mule racing was popular were Rosedale and Greenwood. Karen Glenn writes that mule races were held at Walter Sillers Memorial Park in conjunction with the first Plantation Festival there in 1938. The Rosedale races continued annually until World War II and resumed in 1946.

In Greenwood the Junior Women's Auxiliary organized their mule race to raise money for their charity projects. Those races continued right through the war years until 1948. After that the Jaycees sponsored the races through the 1950s and 1960s.

Kentucky's Ellis Park Racetrack held an event called the Plug Horse Derby. It was a family day with all sorts of contests. Of ten "plug horse" races held in 1951, several were mule races.

Mule racing continues today to be a popular sport under the jurisdiction of the American Mule Racing Association.

The Mule Trading Business

In 1822, mule trading began to be big business in the United States; William Becknell led an expedition to Mexico to buy mules and donkeys to sell to people moving west. Breeders bought the donkeys and began to breed mules for resale. Missouri was the hub of mule breeding and selling, providing thousands of mules for the wagon trains west because it was on the Santa Fe Trail trade route. The mules were sold to transport goods along the Trail.

The cotton, mining, and logging industries provided further markets for mules. By 1870 Missouri had the largest number of mules of all the states.

Guyton and Harrington Mule Company of Kansas had sale barns in Lathrop, Missouri, at the turn of the twentieth century. When World War I created a demand for mules in Britain, they came to Missouri to buy American mules. Neutrality laws made this illegal; when the government found out, Guyton and

Replica of Motlow Mule Sale Poster.

Harrington simply shipped the mules to Canada, selling them as the personal property of Sir Charles Gunning, a British officer. Thousands of mules filtered through Lathrop from all over the country, filling huge barns and creating a mule-based economy.

An interesting name connected to the mule trade is Jack Daniel, who was known for his hot temper. That temper was his undoing; in a fit of anger because he'd forgotten the combination to his safe, he hauled off and kicked the safe. Jack Daniel was diabetic, and the foot injury never healed. As his health deteriorated, Daniel, who never married or had children, turned the distillery business over to his nephew Lem Motlow.

All went well in the whiskey business for Motlow until Prohibition closed all the distilleries. When that happened, Motlow decided to go into the mule business and started an auction in Lynchburg, Tennessee. His business turned into one of the biggest mule markets in the South. He became very rich, and the business thrived until well after World War I.

Atlanta, Georgia, also had a thriving mule business. A *New York Times* article dated February 2, 1880, reports that thousands of the finest mules in the world came to Atlanta. They arrived by the trainload, in top condition from farms in

Tennessee and Kentucky. From Atlanta they were taken throughout Georgia, Alabama, South Carolina, and Florida.

The writer said, "The mule trade of Atlanta brings hundreds of thousands of dollars here every winter and spring."

Mules in the Military

From the time of the American Revolution, mules have been useful, even invaluable, to the military. The United States Army used them extensively during the second Seminole War in the 1850s. Wagons could not be used in the swampy Florida terrain, so instead pack mules were used to transport men and supplies. Mules were also used in the Mexican War and the Indian wars of the 1800s. The fact that mules were hardier than horses in harsh conditions, more surefooted in rough terrain, and could survive on less food and water made them more desirable than the horse. It also made them more expensive to purchase.

General George Crook, who had a thirty-eight-year career with the United States Army, fighting in the Civil War and later in the Indian wars, was known for his dependence on the mule to maneuver supplies and soldiers for fighting Indians. Wagons were not as practical as pack strings. Crook was very particular about the care of the mules and how they were packed. He ordered that they be packed lighter than regulations called for. He often inspected the mules himself. He preferred small Mexican-bred mules to the large draft types. The Mexican mules had better conformation, were more sure-footed, and held up better carrying heavy loads. He in fact set a standard for civilian packers as his reputation spread. Crook also rode a mule, as did some of his staff. Crook's mule packers get credit for the tradition of shaving green mules' tails so they could be distinguished from seasoned mules.

In the Civil War the Union Army found mules indispensable in getting troops, weapons, and supplies from one place to another. The Army purchased more than one million mules during the war. Part of the reason for buying that many mules was to keep them out of the hands of the enemy. The Union bought all mules, regardless of their suitability, from mule traders to prevent the Confederates from getting them. Mules were preferred over horses because they were less likely to contract diseases or suffer from the harsh conditions of war. An enormous amount of food had to be transported to support the mules, even though they could subsist on less feed than horses, so even more mules were needed to haul the food for the mules.

In contrast, Confederate soldiers had to provide their own mules. And while the South had more mules than the North, they did not have mules to spare, since the mules were also needed on farms to raise food and commercial crops like cotton and tobacco. Without mules the economy of the South could not survive. The Confederate Army began the war with a superior cavalry but was not able to replenish the mules and horses lost in battle. Nor did they have the means to provide hay and grain to feed the animals, since the mules that would normally be used on the farm for harvesting had been commandeered into military service.

However, at the end of the war the Northern army had a surplus of mules. General William T. Sherman is credited with promising the freed slaves "forty acres and a mule," an order that was effective only for the first year following the end of the war.

World War I

Britain purchased 115 mules from Guyton and Harrington, the mule brokers headquartered in Lathrop, Missouri, during the Boer War in South Africa between 1898 and 1901. When they entered World War I, they again turned to the same mule trading company. Guyton and Harrington supplied the British with 350,000 mules and horses during that war.

Mules endured the transatlantic journey better than the horses. While horses were lost to disease and stresses associated with close quarters, mules were resistant to shipping fever and other ailments along the way.

Mules and horses were used to pull wagons loaded with supplies and weapons and to carry soldiers into the worst battles. The British were talented in equine management and veterinary care, more so than the American soldiers. When America entered the war, the United States Army lost 23,000 head of mules and horses because they did not have veterinarians to take care of them. The French and British, worried the American stock would infect their own domestic and military animals, volunteered the use of their veterinary hospitals to heal the sick and wounded mules and horses. The Americans bought remounts from France after losing thousands of the animals they shipped in from home.

Many mules were killed in battle or died of fatigue and disease during the worst of the war. Convalescent Horse Depots were created for those that needed veterinary care, rest, and treatment for external parasites. Most of the animals recovered while at the depots and were put back into active service, but nearly 300,000 horses and mules died by the end of World War I. Those that survived were surely the fittest and strongest. Some of those survivors remained in military service, but most were sold as work animals or to slaughterhouses.

World War II

When the United States first entered World War II, the army did not think pack animals were needed. But they soon discovered they were wrong and began to buy horses and mules in large quantities to ship overseas. According to author Emmett M. Essin in his book *Shavetails and Bell Sharps*, by 1943 the military stopped buying horses and purchased only mules. The lack of roads and muddy conditions made the use of horse-drawn wagons obsolete. Mules were better suited for the pack trains used to carry supplies and artillery through the treacherous terrain.

Essin tells us that mule ships held between 300 and 400 mules each. Feed and water had to be carried below deck and the manure up the steps. The manure was held on deck until after dark and then tossed overboard so enemy submarines would not see it.

First Lieutenant Don L. Thrapp, Q.M.C., gave a great deal of information on the value of mules in his *Quartermaster Review* of May–June, 1946. He reported on what was called the Mars Task Force, which took place in Burma. He said the mules were taken off a ship, sent by train, and then by foot over a 300-mile road to Myitkyina. The mules arrived without shoes and in bad condition. The first job was to get the mules in shape for duty. Saddles had to be fitted, sick mules seen to, and, of course, all had to be shod. The mules were classified according to the jobs that suited their conformation and disposition best—draft types for pulling and the smaller ones for packing and riding.

It was the job of the mulemen to take care of the mules at the end of the day. They fed and allowed the animals to graze at least two hours before being rubbed down and picketed for the night. When grazing was not available, they sometimes fed the mules bamboo or banana leaves.

In addition to mules, the operation also acquired two elephants. Thrapp wrote, "A mule can get used to almost anything, but he draws the line at an animal that hangs at both ends. Sensible, not knowing whether an elephant is coming or going, the mule is inclined to play it safe and take off, regardless of road, underbrush, leader, column, or common courtesy."

The mulemen were not always experienced in handling mules. Thrapp wrote that if left to follow, the mules did better than when led by a man. "The average mule is one of the most intelligent and certainly one of the most sure-footed animals in the world. He can see a trail where a man can see nothing but rock. If left to his own devices he will never stumble, rarely slip or bog himself down, and almost never hurt himself." He went on to say, "We occasionally lost animals over the side of mountains, in rivers or bogs, but we never would have lost not a single one had they been free to choose their own way."

While extolling the virtues of the mule, Thrapp admitted, "The sweetest tempered mule knows how to kick and is glad to do it, and for weeks we had more casualties from mules than from Japs."

No mules were shipped back to the United States after the war ended. They were turned over to Europeans to dispose of as they saw fit. Again, many were slaughtered for food. Others were used as work animals on farms and in pack trains. In China most of the mules were shot because some tested positive for equine infectious anemia, an incurable disease transmitted by biting insects.

The United States Army kept a few mules for training. They were brought back into service during the Korean War, after which the army did away with the mule units for about fifty years. Today, however, mules are again serving the military in the Middle East. The bottom line is that these hardy, sure-footed, and intelligent animals can go places no mechanized vehicle can go.

Jockey Jesse Perez guides Idaho Gem to a win in his first race at Winnemucca, Nevada, in June 2006. Idaho Gem was leased by Post Falls, Idaho, businessman Don Jacklin, American Mule Racing Association president, who supported mule cloning research, too. Perez also rode Idaho Star, the youngest of the University of Idaho's three mule clones, to a win in the first race in the series of three Humboldt Futurity trials that day at Winnemucca. Idaho Gem raced competitively in 2007 as well, winning races at California's Humboldt County and Los Angeles County Fairs.   University of Idaho/© Phil Schofield

Cloning

Mules made scientific history in 2003, when the first cloned mule was born on May 4 at Idaho State University. Idaho Gem was also the first hybrid to be cloned. Later two more cloned mules were born. Researchers used a cell from a mule fetus and an egg from a horse to clone Idaho Gem. Later that year Idaho Star was born.

Since mules cannot reproduce, cloning gives hope of preserving the genes of outstanding mule athletes. This is especially interesting to those in the mule racing industry, which hopes cloning will make it possible to preserve the genes of outstanding racers. Cloning mammals also offers the possibility of advances in cancer research.

Idaho Gem and his brother Idaho Star were trained for racing. They won their first race, which was held at the Winnemucca Mule Races in June 2006. The pair placed first and second in a 350-yard sprint, with Idaho Star clocking .027 seconds faster than his brother. Both beat the field of six non-cloned mules. Another cloned mule was born at Idaho State University. It was kept at the university for research while the other two raced.

Mules in the Arts

Mules, with their expressive eyes and long ears, have been models for artists and photographers around the world. The painting of Columbus riding a white mule by A. G. Heaton is one example. Mules often show up in editorial cartoons and modern works of art. Their reputation for stubbornness may explain their popularity in political cartoons. The popular *Snuffy Smith* Sunday comic drawn by John Rose includes Snuffy's mule, Aunt Sukey, in several strips. Mules have starred in films and been the subject of literature and song. You don't have to think hard to remember some very famous mules.

Francis the Talking Mule is probably America's most famous mule. Francis starred in seven movies during the early 1950s. The Francis character was an old Army mule whose sidekick was a young soldier named Peter Stirling, played by Donald O'Connor. Francis got Peter out of trouble by talking good "mule sense" to him—and only him. This led to hilarious consequences when Peter tried to let others know about Francis's unique talent.

Francis's real name was Molly, because "he" was a she. Trainer Les Hilton used a thread fed into Molly's mouth to get her to "talk." Molly worked her lips and mouth trying to spit out the thread, and the words were dubbed in to make it appear as though Francis were talking to Peter. Francis was also the title character in a comic strip during the later 1950s. Today the old movies have been released on video and DVD.

Another famous mule, whose name is often forgotten, is Ruth. Festus, played by Ken Curtis, rode Ruth into Dodge City in the long-running television series *Gunsmoke*. Curtis replaced Dennis Weaver, who played deputy sheriff Chester Goode. Anyone who watched the series can remember Festus fussing and grumbling at "Ole Ruth," who was shown to possess the stereotypical trait of mule stubbornness. But there was no mistaking the affection that they felt for each other.

A mule named Gus starred in a Disney movie by that same name in 1976. Gus played a football team's mascot that got promoted to team member because of his kicking ability, bringing the losing team to victory.

One of the most famous real mascot mules was called Old Coaly. Coaly moved from Kentucky to Pennsylvania in 1857 as a two-year-old. He was brought to work on the campus of Pennsylvania State University by his owner's son, Andy Lytle. Coaly worked hauling limestone to build "Old Main." After the building was finished, Coaly was purchased for $190 and continued to work on campus and surrounding farms. He was loved by the staff and students and became an unofficial mascot. After he died in 1893, his skeletal remains were preserved and are still on display at Penn State.

The mule's qualities and flaws have also been depicted in song. Jimmy Rogers wrote the "Mule Skinner's Blues" in 1930. The ballad tells of a poor mule skinner who is asking the captain for a job. "I Had a Mule" is a folk song about an aggravating, kicking mule, and "Mule Train" was a popular country/western song.

Mules have been the inspiration for many folk tales. "Getting the Mule's Attention" is an old favorite based on the mule's reputation for stubbornness. "The Mule Egg" pokes fun at a city slicker who comes to Kansas to be a farmer. A neighbor convinces him the best way to get a mule is to hatch it from a mule egg. The neighbor gives the novice farmer a coconut, telling him it is a mule egg, and he must sit on it night and day for three weeks to hatch it. The farmer's family and he take turns sitting on the egg and finally decide it is a dud. They throw it into the bushes with disgust. Out jumps a long-eared jackrabbit. The farmer tries to catch the "baby mule" but returns home empty-handed, the rabbit being too fast for him. The farmer's family runs out to see if he caught the baby mule. The farmer says, "No. And it's just as well 'cause I don't want to plow that fast anyway!"

CHAPTER TWO

Mule Types and Equine Hybrids

When bred together, horses and donkeys produce unique members of the equine family—mules and hinnies. Mules are the offspring of a mare (female horse) and a jack (male donkey.) Donkeys, also known as asses, are members of the equus family *Equus asinus*. They vary in size from the tallest Mammoth to the small Mediterranean donkey. Donkeys are native to Africa but can now be found all over the world. They were domesticated around 4000 BCE as beasts of burden. Donkeys of Spanish descent found in the Southwest of the United States are usually called *burros*, which is simply a Spanish word for donkey.

Mules and hinnies are likely to inherit traits from their donkey side that make them different from horses and different from each other. Some of these donkey traits are obvious. They have longer ears and coarser hair, particularly the mane and tail hair. Donkeys have a more vertical pelvis and smaller hooves; they do not have chestnuts on the hind legs; and the ergots of the donkey are much larger than on the horse. Other differences in the donkey that may be passed on to the mule are important but not so visible. In the male donkey, the scrotal skin is thicker and the scrotal blood vessels are larger. For this reason castration can cause excessive bleeding. Donkeys have smaller nasal passages and their larynx is slightly different, which is why donkeys bray and horses whinny, while the mule makes a noise someplace in between.

Donkeys metabolize drugs differently than horses. This trait can be passed on to the mule or hinny offspring. Increased quantity of a drug delivered at shorter intervals may be necessary to have the same effect on a mule or hinny as a horse.

Mules and hinnies can also inherit the donkey's high pain threshold. This is a concern because symptoms are not as apparent and can remain undetected, especially in cases like colic and founder.

Donkey and mule pasture mates.

Hinnies are mules in reverse; they are the offspring of a jennet (female donkey) and a stallion (male horse). As with mules, many opinions and myths, which may or may not be true, surround hinnies. It is not easy to separate the truths about hinnies from the untruths, because very little scientific research has been done on them.

Many sources say hinnies are less popular than the mule, either because they are more horse-like, smaller, or less hardy. For that reason mules are more common than hinnies. But Cynthia Attar, author of *The Mule Companion*, and Amy K. McLean, a writer whose family owns Sowhatchet Mule Farm in Georgia, both say that today's hinnies look pretty much like mules. When in a lineup with mules, hinnies can usually only be distinguished by their slightly shorter ears.

Other factors account for the discrepancies among mule and hinny populations. One is that we have fewer donkeys in the United States than we do horses. Therefore, one male donkey can be bred to many mares, but when you reverse the formula, a limited number of available jennets exist to breed with a stallion.

In addition to fewer available jennets to breed, it is said to be harder to breed for a hinny because the donkey has sixty-two chromosomes and the horse has sixty-four. When a male has more chromosomes than a female, as is the case with stallions and jennets, it is harder for the mare to become pregnant. Attar writes that research done by Cambridge and Cornell universities showed only a 14.4 percent conception rate resulted from 159 attempts in successive breeding seasons to breed 51 jennets. Researchers used a total of six pony and horse stallions in the experiment. Both the jennets and stallions were tested and found to be fertile.

Fertility of Mules and Hinnies

Mules and hinnies are almost always sterile because they have an odd number of chromosomes, having inherited sixty-four from the horse and sixty-two from the donkey so that offspring have sixty-three. The molly (female) mule does exhibit estrus cycles, and because the john (male) mule produces testosterone, but not sperm, it will act like a stallion. For this reason male mules should be gelded. Nevertheless, there are documented cases of mules producing offspring.

One of the rare cases of a mule giving birth occurred in the 1920s. A mule named Old Beck had a female foal that was called Kit. Old Beck passed on a complete set of her genes to her foal. Texas A&M was interested in the case and bought Kit. She was bred to a male horse, and her offspring from that mating was a male horse. She was bred later to a donkey, but she aborted. The fetus was deformed but showed the characteristics of a mule.

Imagine Larry and Laura Amos's surprise when they looked out their window to see a little addition to their mule herd. Mr. and Mrs. Amos own and operate Winter Hawk Outfitters in Collbran, Colorado. They use mules to pack clients

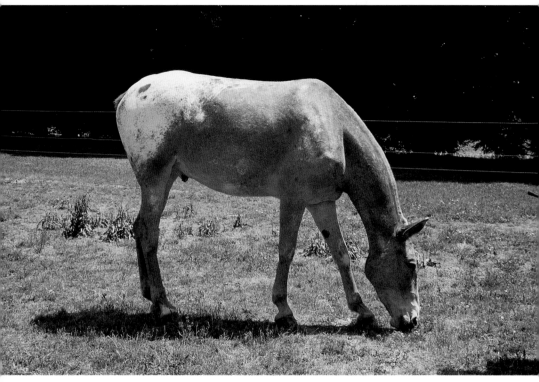
Saddle type mule.

into the wilderness for hunting and fishing trips. On that morning in April 2007, their mule, Kate, apparently gave birth to a foal.

They bought Kate from Randy Pulliam in Arkansas in 2006. They checked with Pulliam right away. He surmised the sire of the foal had to have been his jack, which he'd pastured with Kate and some horses. Larry and Laura had DNA tests run to verify that Kate was indeed the foal's dam. Further tests are being done to establish the foal's species.

Mules and Hinnies in All Sizes

Mules and hinnies come in as many models as there are horses and donkeys to crossbreed. Over the years some general classifications have been adopted that, for the most part, relate to the mule's size or use.

Miniature mule owned and photographed by Susan Morgan, Painted Promise Ranch and Miniature Equine Rescue.

It is safe to say that most mules today are of the saddle, or light, type. Most of these are bred from the light horse breeds by either a standard or Mammoth jack, the largest of donkeys, and are used for riding. Saddle mules can be found on trail rides, in show arenas, and in many "backyard" stables as pleasure mounts.

Less numerous in America is the pony mule. Standing a maximum 14.2 hands, the pony mule results from crossing a pony or small horse with small jacks. These are ideal for pulling carts or as pack animals and are still used for those purposes in some countries. Children and small adults also use them for riding.

Miniature mules, which measure thirty-eight inches or under at the withers, are the result of crossing miniature horses with miniature Mediterranean jacks. They are becoming popular, along with the miniature horse, as exotic pets and as show and driving animals.

Belgian draft mule.

Some mule classifications are throwbacks to the days when mules were primarily work animals. The cotton mule, used on cotton and tobacco farms, weighed 750 to 1,100 pounds and stood 14 to 16 hands.

The sugar mule, a draftier-type mule, was larger than the cotton mule, averaging 1,100 to 1,200 pounds. They were used in the sugar industry for plowing fields, hauling the cane in from the fields, and transporting it to processing factories, either by packing out the bundles of cane or pulling wagons loaded with the sweet harvest. In some cases where no railroads or factories were close to the farm, roads were built for mule trains to transport the cane.

Some small cane farmers made syrup on their property. The mule was the power source that ran the sugar mill. Hooked to a long pole, the mule was sometimes led by the farmer's children in circles to turn the mill. The cane was crushed in the presser, extracting the syrup, which then ran into a pan.

Small mules, called mine mules, were used in gold and coal mines during the first half of the twentieth century. The mules pulled cars of ore from the mines. In some cases they were stabled underground, some serving for up to thirty years without seeing the light of day. They had excellent veterinary care, as it was said that the mule was more valuable to the mining companies than human laborers.

Mules earned their reputation as being stubborn or cantankerous largely in the mining industry. Some say they had the ability to count the number of cars hooked together to be pulled. If they considered the train of ore cars to be more than they could handle, they stood their ground and refused to move until the load was lightened.

Several stories exist about mules that learned to push a miner up against the wall of the mine in tight places to beg for a treat out of the miner's lunch-box, or to even settle a score with an abusive handler. Some miners were killed by well-placed kicks to the head. Mine mules were replaced by automation in the 1960s.

Draft mules are bred out of the draft horse breeds. They usually weigh 1,200 to 1,600 pounds and stand over 15 hands. They were used to pull heavy farm equipment and to haul heavy wagonloads of goods across the country, and they worked in the logging industry before mechanization. Today draft crosses are used for driving heavy wagons and in sports like dressage and jumping.

Zebra Hybrids

Zebras crossed with donkeys or horses are perfect examples of man's desire to play around with Mother Nature. A cross between the male zebra and female horse is called a *zorse,* or zebra mule; if crossed with a pony, the offspring is called a *zony.* A cross between a male zebra and female donkey is a *zebrass.* A female zebra crossed with a stallion is a *hebra,* and the offspring of a female zebra and male donkey is called a *zebret.* The zorse will take on more of the conformation of the horse and the base color of the horse parent, with the strongest stripes on the legs, face, and hindquarters. The zonkey will most closely resemble the donkey in conformation and color. Stripes appear across the hips and faintly on the body, then strongly on the face; the legs have strong stripes with a white background, very much like the zebra parent.

How long ago humans began to experiment with crossbreeding zebras and horses is not certain. It is unlikely to have occurred in the wild, since horses did not survive well in Africa, the natural habitat of zebras. Zebras have a natural immunity to most of the equine diseases that are deadly to the horse and flourish in that continent.

In 1944 explorer Raymond Hook captured a Grevy's zebra stallion and crossed it with mares to use as pack animals for exploring Mount Kenya. The zebra hybrid was an experiment in Africa, offering hope of producing a sturdy work animal resistant to disease, just as the Industrial Revolution made the hoped-for worker unnecessary. Hook found another market for his zorses by selling them to zoos all over the world. In 1955 one of Hook's zorses was exhibited at "Africa USA" in Florida.

Several European zoologists tried crossing the zebra with horses and donkeys. One noted zoologist was Cossar Ewart, professor of natural history in Edinburgh, Scotland. He crossed horse and pony mares of various breeds with a Burchell's zebra stallion. His purpose was two-fold: to produce a disease-resistant hybrid for use in Africa and to test the theory of telegony. Telegony was the theory that a sire could influence the inherited traits of subsequent offspring from the same dam by another sire. This belief was reinforced by experiments done by Lord Morton. In the early 1800s Morton bred a horse mare to a zebra stallion, which resulted in a striped foal. Later he bred the mare to a horse stallion, and the foal exhibited some striping on its legs.

The United States government also carried out similar experimental breeding between horses and zebras. One of those experiments was documented in "Genetics in Relation to Agriculture," by E. B. Babcock and R. E. Clausen, in 1918. These matings showed the telegony theory to be unfounded.

Quagga Project

The *quagga* was striped on its front half and solid brown in the back half, looking like a cross between a zebra and a donkey. DNA from stuffed quagga show the animal was a variant of the plains zebra rather than a hybrid. Unfortunately the quagga was extinct by the late 1800s. Hunters exterminated the animal to leave more grazing room for domesticated livestock. Lord Morton is said to have crossed a male quagga with an Arabian mare, and Charles Darwin referred to this hybrid experiment in several of his writings.

The Quagga Project was started in 1987 by a group of researchers in South Africa. The purpose is to re-create the quagga by selectively breeding plains zebras. In 2005 a foal named Henry was born from the project that closely resembles the original quagga, giving more hope to the Quagga Project.

Modern Zebra Hybrids

Zebra hybrids are gaining in popularity in America. The zebra's colorful stripes make them a favorite among exotic animal collectors and horse folk who want something unique. Some are breeding the endangered Grevy zebra for zoos in hopes of preserving the species. Many of these breeders also breed zebra hybrids, crossing them with donkeys and horses. Some breeders have carried the experimentation further by crossing the zebra with pinto or Appaloosa horses, resulting in a colorful hodgepodge of spotted and striped offspring.

Rowdy and Maggie Bartel own Bartel's Livestock in Grand Junction, Colorado, where they raise zebras and zebra hybrids, in addition to horses and camels. They say the market is good for quality zebra hybrids, with an emphasis on quality. The Bartels estimate the market price for zebra hybrids runs anywhere from $500 to $15,000. They began their breeding program in 1990 when zebra crosses were rare and the market was stronger. Rowdy looks for big, leggy, "good minded" Quarter Horse or Thoroughbred mares with correct feet, legs, and conformation. He wants his zorses to be athletic and beautiful, with stamina, and he stresses the importance of them being "good minded."

Bartel says, "I have decided that where a bad zorse or mule comes from is people who say, 'That mare doesn't deserve to be bred to our stallion; she needs a donkey or zebra jack,' and they breed her to one or the other. If your mare doesn't have good horse babies, you are wasting your time breeding her to a zebra."

The Bartels find zorses are not for everyone, but they are very trainable by someone who knows how to train horses or mules. The Bartels have trained their zorses and zonkeys for both riding and packing.

Like the other equine hybrids, mules and hinnies, the zebroid will inherit physiological differences from its zebra parent. With little research to rely on, breeders are for the most part experimenting when they crossbreed zebras with horses and donkeys. Stephanie Hemphill sums it up in her booklet *Zebra Mules*: "While some breeders have had a great deal of success in the past and have been very proud of their animals, others have failed and have been very disappointed."

CHAPTER THREE

Preparing for Ownership: Housing, Transportation, and Equipment

Because mules come in sizes from miniature to draft types, living quarters will depend on what kind of mule is being purchased. The size of the barn, outbuildings, and the turnout space all depend on the size and number of mules being kept. The mule's purpose as well as the geographic location will also have some bearing. A pleasure or work mule will do fine with a run-in shed for its shelter in temperate climates, while a show animal may need a barn with a stall and a wash area.

The important thing is to plan carefully. First check the zoning, which may prohibit using the property for livestock. Find out if there are any environmental regulations, easements, deed restrictions, or covenants on the state, county, or local levels.

If the all-clear is given, next select the best layout for the facility, including the location of shelters, storage buildings, paddocks, and pastures. Consider access, drainage, convenience to water and electricity sources, and room for expansion.

Shelter

In his book *Horses and Horsemanship,* M. E. Ensminger writes, "Horses kept in an open shed, even in colder areas, are healthier and suffer fewer respiratory diseases than horses kept in an enclosed barn." This goes for mules as well. Keeping mules at pasture not only has physical and mental benefits, it is less expensive for the owner. For those reasons, unless the mule needs to be

A barn with stalls offers the owner convenience.

confined for health reasons or the animal is being shown, it just makes good sense to let him live outdoors, with a run-in shed to offer adequate shelter from the elements.

The shed must be in the right location to provide the intended benefits. It should have good surface drainage, be convenient for the owner to access, and face away from prevailing winds.

The size of the shed depends on the size and number of mules. The rule of thumb is sixty to eighty square feet per 1,000-pound mule. The shed should be at least twenty-four feet deep to offer protection from wind, rain, and snow. The front height should be at least ten feet and the back eight feet for the average-sized mule. Large draft types will need a fourteen by fourteen-foot stall. An eight by eight-foot stall is adequate for a miniature mule.

An open front shed is the most common design. The roof and sides are not usually insulated unless to prevent condensation. Condensation can occur when the air inside the stable, warmed by the animals' body heat, comes in contact with cold inside walls or ceiling. Leave an opening between the top of the back wall and the roof for cross ventilation. Dropdown panels placed in the back and sides can increase ventilation in summer and then be closed in the winter. A partially closed front can provide added protection in colder climates.

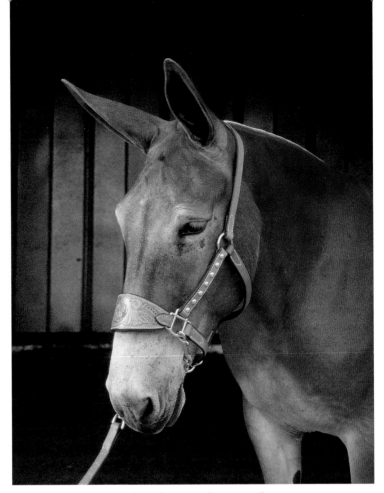
Mules like to have plenty of ear clearance when in a stall.

A simple Quonset-style hut made from heavy tarp stretched over a frame is easy and inexpensive to either construct or buy ready-made. It works well for a small or miniature mule and has the added advantage of being portable.

A barn with stalls for more than one mule offers the owner convenience. It is easier to feed several mules at once when they can be confined to individual stalls. Mules that are performing or being shown can be kept cleaner in a stall, and if one is sick or has been injured it can be confined. A tack room, feed room, and wash area are additional features that make a barn desirable.

Unique to housing mules is the need for enough ear clearance. Some mules are sensitive about anything touching their ears. If the ceiling is too low, they will stand with their heads dropped to avoid letting their ears touch the top of the stall.

Outbuildings

When planning the overall facility, take into account which outbuildings in addition to the barn or run-in shed will be needed. Most experts recommend storing hay in a separate enclosed building, not the barn, because hay is so flammable. Hay is sometimes stored overhead in a barn, but that increases dust and mold in the stalls below, which can cause respiratory problems in the mules living there.

Other outbuildings to consider are shelters for tractors, trailers, and other equipment; a compost bin for manure; storage for bedding; and a riding arena or round pen. All of these structures should be mapped out in the preliminary plan. Consider convenience, accessibility, space, and esthetics when designing the facility.

Fences and Gates

Good fences are the key to keeping the mule home and out of trouble. Budget, labor, esthetics, and above all safety determine the type of fence to use. The number of mules, amount of available space, and placement of the buildings help determine how much fencing is needed. The size of the mule will be a deciding factor in the height of the fences, and the amount of exercise room the animal will need will determine the amount of fencing needed. Fences for saddle-type mules should be at least five feet tall, and six feet for draft mules. When building a fence for miniature mules, be sure they cannot crawl under the fence.

There are a variety of fencing materials and designs to choose among. Wood, steel pipe, PVC, and woven wire are some of the most commonly used materials for fences. Barbed wire and high tensile wire should be avoided, since the mule can become entangled and sustain severe injuries. Many farm owners will use a more attractive and expensive fence in the front of the property and less-expensive fencing material at the back where passersby cannot see it. Dr. Bob Mowrey, Extension Horse Specialist at North Carolina State University, writes in his article "Selecting Fences for Horses" that "No fence at all may be better than a fence in poor repair." He recommends that owners consider whether they have the expertise and time to install their own fence or if they can afford a professional contractor to install it. He points out that, "Large fenc-

Good fences are the key to keeping the mule home and out of trouble.

ing projects can be long and tedious." He also notes that future maintenance and whether the materials will be available in the future must be considered.

The gate to the paddock or pasture must be secure, safe, and easy to operate. The gate should be wide enough to drive a truck and tractor through. It must be able to withstand the abuse the mule will inflict on it by leaning on the gate, running into it, kicking it, or grazing underneath it. Remember that often you will be leading your mule with one hand and need to be able to open and shut the gate with the other. A heavy, long gate will be more difficult to handle and will need extra support to prevent warping and sagging. One solution is to mount a wheel on the bottom corner to keep the gate from dropping to the ground. This will make opening and closing it easier. Another way to support long gates is to attach a cable from the upper corner of the opening end to the

The gate to the paddock or pasture must be secure, safe, and easy to operate.

top of a higher post at the hinged end. A turnbuckle placed at the center of the cable will allow you to take up any slack in the cable caused by stretching.

Keep in mind that some mules have a real talent for opening gates and can manage almost any sort of latch. The slide stick latch is a commonly used closure. The problem with this latch is it is as easy for mules to operate as for humans. The hook and chain latch is better. Wrapping the chain around the post and the gate, then securing it with a snap is usually enough to outsmart most mules. In addition, position the latch out of reach of the mule.

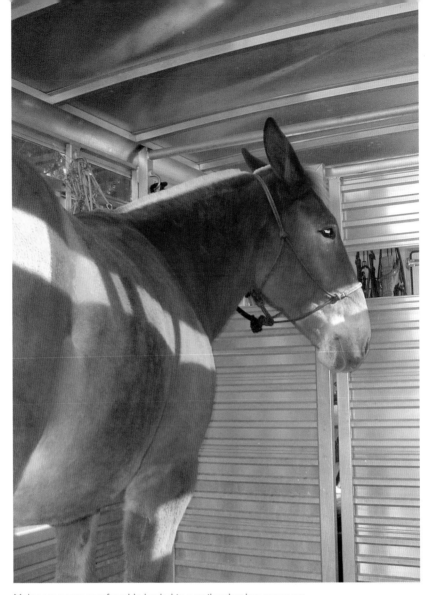

Mules are more comfortable hauled in a trailer that has ear room.

Transportation

The standard horse or stock trailer is suitable for transporting the average mule. If the mule is of the draft type, a larger, heavy-duty trailer will be needed, with extra floor support, heavy-duty tires, and a wider, stronger axle. As with a stall, a mule will be more comfortable being hauled in a trailer that has ear room.

Trailer maintenance is the key to hauling mules safely. Before every trip, inspect the tires and brakes. Be sure the floorboards are sound and check them for rot. Replace boards as needed. The lights inside and outside the trailer should be in good working order. Be sure there are no protruding screws, bolts, or anything else that can injure the mule and that the door latches and hinges are sturdy.

At least annually, check and make needed repairs to framing and construction of the trailer. Look for rust and other damage. Have the wiring and lights inspected. Check the wheels and tires, the ramp, and the doors.

Rubber floor mats help prevent the mule from slipping and absorb sound. Bedding can also be added to make cleaning the trailer easier. The bedding and mats should be removed after hauling and the floor cleaned thoroughly to prevent rotting.

Certain state and federal regulations require a commercial license if the towing vehicle, trailer, and load exceed 10,000 pounds. The weight of one draft mule can equal that of two light mules, so it is important to check towing weight. This can be done at a grain elevator. There are restrictions in various states regarding height, weight, and length of the towing rig. Check with the department of transportation to learn your state's regulations. Always heed the sign at weigh stations even if you know you are properly licensed and weigh under the legal limit, because they are also used to check health papers, Coggins tests, registration papers, and drivers' licenses. Not doing so can result in stiff penalties.

Tack, Harness, and Equipment

What the mule will be doing will determine what sort of equipment will be needed. The mule is versatile; some are ridden English while others go Western. Even within those disciplines there are saddle decisions to make: synthetic or leather; adjustable tree, flex tree, or no tree at all; close contact, all-purpose, or endurance; and the list goes on.

Since mules come in various shapes and sizes, saddle fit will be a concern. Several companies make Western saddles with trees especially designed for the mule's back, which tends to be straight. Some mules may have a slight con-

Breeching keeps the saddle from sliding forward.

vex lift to the spine, whereas the horse's back is normally slightly concave. In case the saddle slides forward, many riders also use a crupper or breeching to keep the saddle from putting pressure on the mule's withers and neck when going downhill. Some riders prefer mohair string girths because they wick away moisture from sweating, which helps prevent girth sores. A back girth is used to keep the saddle from tilting up when riding in hilly terrain. It is important that all the rigging fits snugly to prevent slipping, which will cause saddle sores. Buckles and straps should be checked every time they are used, both because the mule's weight changes and strapping stretches.

The old-time Western look is popular with mule riders.

Because some mules have an aversion to having their ears handled, bridling can be a problem. There are bridles on the market that have a snap-over-the-ear browband so the handler can bridle the mule without having to tuck the ears between the crownpiece and browband. Missouri Mule Company also makes a one-ear headstall with a snap-over-ear loop. Heavy, tooled leather halters with a wide noseband are popular when showing mules in hand. According to Shannon Hoffman, longtime mule owner, the most popular style of Western tack is the old-time Western look, with buckaroo boots and chaps for the rider and saddles and bridles that resemble those from the early 1900s or late 1800s.

A plow or driving mule will require a harness. Size, new or used, synthetic or leather are some of the points to ponder when shopping for harness. Many people like nylon or other synthetic harnesses because they are lightweight and can be easily washed with soap and water. However, leather harness is a must when showing.

Keeping tack and equipment clean and in good repair will ensure long life and safe use. Clean off sweat and grime after every use. Nylon equipment can be cleaned with soap and water. Regularly take apart a leather saddle, bridle, harness, or other tack, thoroughly clean with saddle soap, and then apply leather conditioner or oil. Inspect tack for weak spots, tears, and broken hardware. Have repairs made before using the item again. The areas most prone to wear are around the buckles. Readjust the straps so they buckle in a different place to make the tack last longer. Stitching wears out long before the leather or nylon parts. A saddle shop or shoe repair shop can repair stitching.

Finally, store tack in a clean, dry place to prevent mold and mildew, which will damage leather goods. Hang bridles, harness, and other strap goods where they are easy to reach, and keep saddles on a rack or stand. Make sure the tack storage area is not accessible to rats and mice or puppies, because they like to chew on the leather.

CHAPTER FOUR

Buying a Mule

"Do like I did, and talk to a lot of people who know mules before you buy one," advises Shannon Hoffman, who serves on the board of directors of the Carolina Mule Association. That is good advice. If you are a novice, ask a mentor who knows mules to help you in your quest to find the right mule.

Once you have decided to buy a mule, there are some questions you need to ask yourself. The most important is, "What will I want to do with my mule?" As you've learned, mules come in many models, from miniature mules to draft mules. Do you want to show, trail ride, drive, pack, or farm with your mule? Answering this question will narrow the playing field, but there are other questions to answer in the quest for the perfect mule. Are you an experienced horseman? Do you have the proper facility for housing a mule? Can you afford to keep a mule?

Do some research before you begin shopping for your mule. Read ads in mule magazines and ask mule owners what a mule should cost. Many things help determine the mule's value. The equine market changes from year to year, or even with the seasons. Some say the market goes down in the fall because owners are concerned about the cost of keeping a mule through the winter, when pastures are dormant and the cost of hay and feed are up. Age, type or breed-cross, training, location, health, and soundness all factor into the price of mules. Very young mules may cost less initially, but if you are paying for training, that will drive up the cost. If the price seems too good to be true, chances are there is something wrong with the mule.

The auction arena provides a large number of mules to examine at one time in one place, but it is not the best place for a novice to buy a mule. An auction does not give you time to examine the mule or have a vet check it out.

Have a trusted agent or experienced person go with you if you decide to shop at an auction.

A new, high-tech innovation is online bidding at live auctions. You can bid on mules from your home computer if it is linked to a company that specializes in Internet broadcasting and has set up digital cameras focused on the mules in the sale arena at the auction. With live video and audio, people can bid with the click of a mouse even if they are across the country from the live auction. The bidder has to have high-speed Internet service and register and qualify to receive a buyer's number. This saves the expense of traveling to sales, but it is no place for first-time buyers without an agent who really knows the business.

According to Deborah Cox, the one place a novice should not buy a mule is from a used-car dealer. That's where she got her mule named Yahoo. Even though the car dealer assured her that his twelve-year-old son rode the mule regularly, Yahoo turned out to be a bucking handful.

Yahoo's owner, Deborah Cox, bought him from a used car dealer, which is not the best place for a novice to buy a mule.
Photo courtesy of Deborah Cox

"Yahoo wasn't actually standing on the car lot, nor did I trade in a vehicle for him. However, like many car dealers, the seller was less than honest about the 'vehicle' that I was purchasing, and Yahoo didn't have a thirty-day warranty or fall under the New York lemon law. At the time I bought him, they had no place on their property to 'test drive him,' so I took their word for his training level," said Deborah, who is glad she was the one to buy the mule. "A less experienced horse or mule person would have been in big trouble with him, and had I not purchased him, I think that he ultimately would have been a lawn ornament [standing idle in the pasture] or sold at auction."

Bonnie Croft and her husband Tom, of Verona, New York, took a safer route when they bought their first mules. They acquired their mules because they owned a tree nursery and landscaping business. In the spring when the ground was wet and muddy, they needed to get the trees out of the field to give

Bonnie and Tom Croft bought their mules from a reputable mule dealer who let them take the mules on trial before closing the deal.   Photo courtesy of Bonnie Croft

to buyers. A tractor would make terrible ruts and get stuck, so they bought a team of mules to pull the trees out to the loading dock.

They contacted a mule dealer who had a very good reputation, made an appointment, and went to see his mules. Never having owned driving horses or mules, the Crofts watched the dealer catch, harness, and hitch the team to a wagon. Then he drove them, and then Tom drove. All went well. The dealer shipped the mules to the Crofts' farm with the understanding they could try them out, and if they wanted to keep them, they would mail a check. That was thirty years ago.

"You don't find that kind of trustworthiness nowadays," Bonnie said.

The Crofts learned to drive on Mike and Mack. Years later Mack died and they bought Jim. The pair were in their thirties when they died. The Crofts then bought three Belgian horse fillies, raised them to breeding age, and started raising their own mules.

Breeders usually have young stock for sale. The disadvantage of buying young mules is they will need training. If you are an experienced horse owner and have training know-how and the time to get your mule to the place you want it, then a breeder can be a good source for young mules. The parents of the mule will usually be there for inspection, and the breeder can give you the mule's history. Often there will be other mules from the same bloodlines to compare. If you are a novice, you will be better off buying an older, well-trained mule. Leave the youngsters to the more experienced.

Ads and private sales are the most common place for first-time-mule buyers to find the right mule. The key is taking along your mentor to help evaluate the mule. It's never wise to fall in love with the first mule you see. After you've looked at several and found one you really like, go back for a second look.

If you are new to the equine world, an older, more experienced, and well-trained mule is the best choice. Most mules in their early teens have had enough life experience not to be flustered by a beginner's mistakes. However, you don't want an extremely aged mule that will begin to have health problems.

In the article "How to Buy a Mule" in the autumn 2004 issue of *Rural Heritage* magazine, Steve Edwards advises that disposition is everything when picking out a mule. If the mule walks up to you and meets you at the gate, turns and faces you, and is easy to catch and halter, chances are that this mule will be easy to live with. Observe how well the mule leads. It should come along willingly with slack in the lead rope. The mule should also stand quietly and enjoy being groomed, and it should enjoy the conversation going on around it. Edwards says *whoa* is the most important word the mule should know. When it is commanded to whoa, the mule should stop, stand, and wait for further instructions.

Be sure the mule you buy is trained to do what you want to do with it. A driving mule may not always be broke to ride, and one used to pulling with a teammate might not work well alone. Don't take the seller's word for anything, but have him or her demonstrate everything he or she claims the mule knows how to do. If the seller says the mule is good about its feet, have him pick up its feet and then tap the hoof with a hammer. Some mules are fine about having their feet cleaned but may not like to be shod. Have the seller clip the mule's ears if he claims the mule is tolerant of clippers. Have the seller load it on a trailer, drive if it drives, ride if it is saddle broke, or pack it if it was advertised as a good pack animal. Again, don't take anything for granted; the proof is in the doing.

Once you've seen the seller perform with the mule, it's your turn. Touch the mule all over, pick up its feet, and touch its ears. Ride, drive, or plow with it. Before you buy, you should try whatever you plan to do with it once you take it home.

Before you finalize a sale, have your veterinarian perform a pre-purchase exam. This will be at your expense, but it can save you from an costly mistake. It is also a good ideal to have a farrier evaluate the mule. He will check the health of the feet and the mule's attitude about having its feet handled and shod.

If the seller is not the mule's original owner, try to get the names and contact information of previous owners and give them a call. Ask if they had any health or handling problems with the mule. Finally, ask the current owner if a trial period or a lease-to-own option is possible. Insist on a written agreement between the seller and yourself stating all the terms, especially if you take the mule home on trial or you are buying on an installment plan.

CHAPTER FIVE

Health and Care

The mule is known to be a hardy animal with few health problems. This hybrid inherits its donkey sire's ability to withstand heat, its tough hooves made to travel desert and mountain country, and its ability to utilize food efficiently. Being an easy keeper is one reason the mule is gaining so much appeal. Still, even with the mule's hybrid vigor, the owner must follow the basic rules of good equine management to keep the mule healthy and happy.

Nutrition

One of the things that made mules desirable for packing, pulling, and riding during the westward movement was their ability to survive on less food than horses and oxen. In his book *The Mule Alternative,* Mike Stamm quotes from letters and journals of men who made that grueling trip west. Robert Chalmers wrote during the California gold rush, "Poor mules stand the journey, but horses do not, especially if they are large." Lieutenant W. H. Emory, a topographical engineer for the United States Army, wrote on August 4, 1846, "The total distance was thirty-six miles. The horses were now falling away in an alarming manner, but the mules seem to require the stimulus of distention, and nothing else: this the dry grass affords."

Mules, with the exception of pony or miniature mules, seldom overeat to the point of colic or founder, as many horses will. But Shannon Hoffman warns they can still founder from being overweight. She suggests that to prevent the mule from becoming overweight, it is not uncommon to put them in a dry lot during the summer when pastures are lush.

Most mules do fine on a good-quality hay or pasture and need their diets supplemented with grain only when working hard or being shown.

Mules require about one-third less feed than horses of comparable size.

Most mules do fine on a good-quality hay or pasture and need their diets supplemented with grain only when working hard or being shown. An article in *Rural Heritage* magazine by Paul and Betsy Hutchins indicates that a working mule's grain ration is about one-third that of a comparably sized horse.

That mules require smaller rations than horses is also apparent in the United States Army's *Field Manual Special Forces Use of Pack Animals*. In the manual's charts, the mule's ration is less than that for horses, including grain, hay, and even water. The recommended grain ration for horses is ten pounds and for mules eight; horses are fed twelve pounds of hay and mules ten. The average daily water requirement for horses is thirty to fifty liters, and for mules it is fifteen to thirty liters. The manual states, "These guidelines to feeding should only be considered as a starting point." It explains that adjustments should be made to maintain ideal body weight.

Commercial feeds are available in a variety of rations to meet the special needs of young, growing mules that need a higher protein food, as well as high-fat rations for aged mules. For most adult mules being fed a commercial feed, a basic 10-percent protein feed mix is adequate. The amount given depends on the body weight of the mule and the amount of work it is doing. For example,

Waiting for supper.

a mule training for pulling competition will need more feed than one that is trail ridden on the weekends. Rations should be weighed out, not measured according to volume.

Draft mules are susceptible to a disease called equine polysaccharide storage myopathy (EPSM), a condition also found in draft horses, in which glycogen and glycogen-related compounds are stored in the muscles instead of being used as energy. EPSM has various symptoms, including stiff gait, muscle cramps, shivers, azoturia, wasting away of muscles, and weakness. A low-carbohydrate, high-fat diet is the best prevention and treatment for those that have the disease. Because mules require a smaller amount of concentrated feeds, there is less chance they will develop EPSM, but if a mule shows any of the symptoms, a veterinarian should be consulted.

Mules being fed commercial feed will not, under normal circumstances, need additional mineral and vitamin supplements, with the exception of salt. Salt should be available in either block or loose form at all times but not added to the mule's feed.

Water is the most important nutrient. The mule needs access to clean water at all times. The mule's donkey heritage means that it can survive a long time without water, and most will not over drink, even when they have been deprived. This was another feature that made the mule an ideal beast of burden while crossing the deserts of the Old West. It is still a benefit of using mules in the Middle Eastern deserts today.

Ideally, water should be about fifty-five degrees Fahrenheit to be most palatable. In freezing temperatures, break surface ice. This can be accomplished using a hammer to break the ice. Or install a livestock water heater that will keep the water above freezing temperature. In hot weather, care should be taken not to let the water stagnate. Empty the buckets or water trough daily and refill with fresh water to prevent algae growth.

Preventive Health Care

Because of their hybrid vigor, mules have few health problems, but they are susceptible to many of the same diseases as horses. The old saying "an ounce of prevention is worth a pound of cure" is true. Many common equine diseases can be prevented with vaccinations and good management practices. Mules, like their horse cousins, should be vaccinated against sleeping sickness, West Nile, tetanus, strangles, flu, and, in some locations, Potomac Horse Fever. Check with your veterinarian to learn which vaccinations equines in your region need.

Internal parasite infestation causes weight loss, enteritis, peritonitis, colic, and death. The most dangerous of internal parasites are large strongyles, but many other "worms" affect the health of the mule. They include small strongyles, known as bloodworms; ascarids, also known as lungworms or roundworms; pinworms, stomach worms, and tapeworms. Fortunately, a regular deworming program and good hygiene will control internal parasites.

Mules are reported to be more susceptible to ascarids than horses. This parasite is most common in foals because they have not yet developed a resistance to them. Ascarid eggs are picked up in infested pastures. The eggs hatch in the intestine and migrate to the lungs and liver where they cause heavy damage. From there the larvae migrate to the upper respiratory system and are coughed up, then swallowed. The larvae mature in the small intestines. The mature worm, which can reach up to twelve inches in length, can cause a blockage in the intestines, leading to deadly colic or ruptures. Control ascarids by deworming the mule as recommended by your veterinarian.

Dr. Theresa A. Fuess writes that mules are also more susceptible than horses to an external parasite called *habronemiasis*. This is caused by an infestation of the habronema, or stomach worm larvae. Houseflies carry the larvae. The fly lands, feeds on a wound, and then deposits the larvae, which burrow into the wound. The infected wound looks like proud flesh and is known as Jack sores. The sore seems to go away in winter but is actually resting or lying dormant. It will return to an infected state in the spring. Fly control is the best prevention. A veterinarian should be called in to treat the wound, since most topical remedies are not effective.

When considering pasture management to help control parasites, it is important not to overstock the pasture. The rule of thumb is one mule per two acres to prevent overgrazing. Mow and harrow the pasture regularly to expose manure droppings to the sun to reduce parasite eggs. Divide pastures and practice rotational grazing when possible. Separating old and young horses also helps control parasites.

The bot fly is another parasite harmful to all equines. The adult fly lays its eggs on the hairs of the mule. These are swallowed when the mule grooms itself and then hatch into larvae inside the mouth. They stay there about a month, then migrate to the stomach and attach to the stomach lining. There they live for up to a year, causing severe damage. Bots are passed out with feces and then grow to the pupae stage; they mature into an adult fly and repeat the cycle. Remove bot eggs from the mule's hair by scraping them off with sandpaper or a bot removal knife, which you can buy at a tack shop.

Good hygiene is necessary to maintaining the mule's overall health. The mule's environment, whether it is a stall, paddock, or pasture, should be kept clean. Picking out manure and wet bedding from the stall daily reduces bacteria and fly populations. Fumes from ammonia in wet bedding can also cause respiratory disease in the mule. Manure should be removed from stalls and small paddocks daily. Compost the manure before spreading it on a pasture that is being grazed, or spread uncomposted manure on pastures not being used for grazing. Do not feed mules off the ground.

The barn should allow sunlight into the stalls. Sunlight is a deterrent to the growth of bacteria. Grooming the mule regularly produces healthy skin and creates an opportunity for examining the mule for any injuries. Applying insect repellent after grooming reduces external parasite irritations. External parasites, including flies, mosquitoes, ticks, and lice, carry disease and cause skin irritations and mental distress in mules. Following the above instructions for good sanitation and using insect repellents will help control external parasites.

Hoof Care

Mules are known to have strong hooves and can often remain barefoot. Their feet are anatomically different from horses: Hooves are long and narrow, with less angle, and are generally more elastic and tougher, which makes them less likely to crack and chip.

Clean hooves daily, and keep the mule in a clean, dry environment. Regular trimming or shoeing by a good farrier, preferably one with mule experience, is necessary to maintain healthy hooves. How often hooves need to be trimmed or shoes reset depends on how fast the hooves grow and how fast they wear down. Rough and rocky ground and paved roads cause excessive wear and tear on the hooves. Mules worked in those conditions will probably need shoes, and the shoes will need changing more often than a mule worked on soft ground. As a rule, a mule's hooves need to be trimmed every six to eight weeks.

A healthy hoof is achieved through good nutrition and can be recognized by the natural gloss on its surface. The healthy frog, a triangular-shaped pad on the bottom of the foot, should be the consistency of a pencil eraser. There should be no separation between the wall and the sole of the foot, as this allows bacteria to reach the sensitive part of the foot.

A common hoof disease is thrush, detected by a strong, foul odor and black discharge in the area of the frog. The best line of defense is prevention through regular hoof cleaning. A mule that does get thrush can be treated with a variety of remedies that can be purchased at tack or farm supply stores. One good home remedy is household bleach applied directly to the infected area. Be sure to wear eye protection when applying any chemical medication to the

Clean the hoof daily.

hoof. From my personal experience, a quick kick or jerk can splash the liquid into the handler's eye, sending him or her directly to the emergency room. One way to avoid accidental spilling is to put the bleach in a squeeze bottle.

Founder is not as common among mules as horses, but it does occur. Founder is a potential result of laminitis, or inflammation of the laminae, the connective tissue that holds the hoof wall to the foot. Many things can cause inflammation of the laminae, including concussion, overeating, being overweight, or any systemic disease that causes a high fever. In the most severe cases, founder can lead to complete separation of the hoof wall, which allows the coffin bone to rotate and drop down to, or even through, the sole of the foot.

Signs of founder are heat and increased digital pulse in the hoof, anxiety in the mule, an exaggerated stance, trembling, and increased respiration, all due to the severe pain this conditions causes. Some mules are very stoic and do not show normal signs of pain until the condition is advanced. A veterinarian should be called at once if founder is suspected. While waiting for the vet, soak the mule's affected foot or feet in ice water to reduce the inflammation. Typical treatment involves drugs to reduce the inflammation and removing the cause of the condition. Chronic cases may require corrective trimming and shoeing.

Abscesses can be a secondary condition of founder or be caused by a bruise. Sometimes a grain of sand or other foreign object works its way from the white line in the hoof wall to the coronet band, where it then ruptures. Once an abscess ruptures, the pain will subside. After the rupture occurs, the wound should be packed with an antibacterial agent and the hole kept packed until it heals. A farrier may be able to lance the abscess. If not, applying a poultice or soaking the foot in Epsom salts will help.

Kicking is an issue worth discussing in hoof care. Mules have a reputation for being likely to kick, especially when their hind feet are handled. They are also reputed to have better aim than their horse cousins. This is an issue that should be dealt with when the mule is a youngster, since its feet must be handled throughout its life. Nothing will drive a good farrier away faster than a kicker.

Dental Care

Have the veterinarian check the mule's teeth annually. Mules' teeth grow continually. In the process of eating, the teeth wear down, but depending on diet, teeth sometimes wear unevenly, causing sharp edges, known as hooks, to form. The sharp edges are painful, especially while the mule is eating, and can interfere if the mule wears a bit. The veterinarian can remedy this problem by floating, or filing, the sharp edges.

Common Equine Ailments

Colic, a symptom rather than a disease, basically means the mule has a bellyache. This can be a mild or deadly condition, depending on its cause and how quickly it is treated. A blockage of the digestive system that causes gas, fluids, or feed to accumulate is a primary cause of colic. Internal parasite infestations cause 90 percent of intestinal blockages. Impaction in the colon and/or caecum can be caused by poor quality roughage, teeth problems that interfere with chewing, or sand ingestion. A twisted or herniated intestine is one of the most serious forms of intestinal obstruction and usually requires surgery.

Because the mule can tolerate more pain than horses, colic may remain undetected. Normal signs of colic pain include craning the neck to look at the side, the typical location of its pain, and even biting at that side. Sweating, increased respiration, pawing, and lying down and rolling are other signs of colic. It is possible that by the time these signs are exhibited, the mule has suffered longer than a horse would before showing typical signs. The vet should be called immediately when colic is suspected. While waiting for the vet, keep the mule on its feet so it cannot lie down and roll. Rolling may cause the intestines to twist and block the intestines and blood flow to the intestines, which will increase the severity of the mule's condition. Sometimes, especially in the case of gas colic, just getting the mule to move around will relieve its pain. In severe cases when there is an obstruction, surgery may be the only alternative. In milder cases, drenching with mineral oil or giving a drug to stimulate the digestive processes will relieve the mule. Quality food, regular deworming programs, clean water, and exercise are the best ways to prevent colic.

Leah Patton, in her article "Healthy as a Horse, Stubborn as a Mule," writes that donkeys and mules are more likely to have sarcoid tumors than horses. Sarcoids are non-cancerous and at first glance look like a wart. They are usually found on the head, especially around the eyelid, but also occur on other parts of the body, and often several of the tumors grow together. Though not known for sure, it is thought a virus causes sarcoids. They can be removed surgically but usually return.

Patton states in her article that donkeys are prone to fatty tumors, or lipomas. They are also found in obese and aged mules. Mules allowed to become overweight get cellulite deposits. One area where this often occurs is the crest. Tumors sometimes occur in gelded mules, which cause them to look intact. These tumors can be removed by surgery. Lipomas also occur inside the abdominal cavity, where they can become entwined with the intestines and cause strangulation colic and, ultimately, death. This is reason enough to not overfeed.

Zebroids require the same attention to health care as mules. Because zebras are resistant to sleeping sickness, early experiments crossing zebras with horses were done in part with the hopes of producing a pack and riding animal that would inherit that resistance. It did not work, and zebra hybrids should be vaccinated against that disease, as well as other common equine diseases.

CHAPTER SIX

Working Mules

For almost two centuries the mule was the mainstay of American farmers, especially in the South. Mules were used for plowing, harvesting, and hauling goods to market. The mule inherited its stamina in hot weather from the desert-bred donkey side of the family, which made the mule a valued work animal on Southern cotton and tobacco farms. In addition to farm work, the mule was important as a pack animal and for pulling wagons in the commercial and military worlds.

Farming

In high-tech and mechanized America, the idea of farming with mules may seem like a step backward, but more and more small farmers are finding the practice cost effective and environmentally friendly. Organic and green farmers are more often using work animals to power plows and cultivators. Advocates suggest that farmers save money not just on fossil fuels, but on the initial cost of buying the animal. Refurbishing vintage equipment is also less expensive than buying and repairing a tractor and modern accessories. The mule isn't likely to need new parts or other expensive repairs. The mule can even help produce its own "fuel"—food, that is.

Some favor mules over horses simply because they are hardier and cheaper to feed. In her article "Following the Plow" in the Spring, 1974, issue of *Mother Earth News,* Gail Damerow writes: "In Southern states, mules are more popular than horses because they can better withstand the South's hot, humid weather." She goes on to say the mule's peripheral vision is better than

Victor Pace at the plow with his mule team, Kate and Kit.   Photo by Shannon Hoffman

that of the horse, making mules less likely to shy. She comments on the mule's sure-footedness and sense of self-preservation as additional pluses.

Tom and Bonnie Croft, as described in Chapter Four, owned a tree nursery and used Belgian draft mules to cultivate and harvest the trees. Tom also used the mules to do "old-fashioned farming." He planted, plowed, and prepared their land for crops and mowed and raked hay with their mules. Tom also enjoyed trying out all the old-fashioned farm equipment.

They started out with experienced mules they bought in Pennsylvania. That was about thirty years ago. From there they bought three Belgian draft mules, bred them to a jack, and began raising their own mules. Bonnie says, "We enjoyed the babies and had a lot of fun, eventually having them trained to drive at the local college draft program." The program Bonnie refers to is the draft horse management curriculum at Morrisville State College in Morrisville, New York.

Today the Crofts have retired. They have gone from working to enjoying their mules. Bonnie shows in driving competitions, training mules by driving around the farm and neighboring land.

The famous Grand Canyon mules have returned from taking visitors on yet another trip down the Bright Angel Trail, Grand Canyon National Park. National Park Service Photo

Tourism

The mule is widely used in the tourist industry. Reese Brothers Mule Company in Gallatin, Tennessee, is one of the United States' largest mule suppliers. It's been in business since the 1920s, when Rufus M. Reese Sr. began the company. Reese Brothers reports on its Web site that it sells up to four hundred mules a year to Grand Canyon Trail Concessionaires. In addition, it sells many to carriage tour companies in the French Quarter in New Orleans, Pennsylvania Amish farmers, and hunt clubs in Georgia.

Mule rides through the Grand Canyon have been popular since 1925, when the Union Pacific Railroad initiated the rides into Western national parks. Today riders can choose between a day trip and an overnight trip. The two-day overnight trip takes them all the way down to the Colorado River. They spend the night in a lodge and trek back the next day. Tourists have to book eleven months ahead to experience a mule ride down the Grand Canyon.

Mule pack trip outfitters and hiking and hunting outfitters also use mules to pack gear. One unique hiking outfitter is Call of the Wild, an eight-day, fifty-eight-mile hike for women in the High Sierras. Women do not have to carry backpacks; the mules pack in all the food and camping gear.

Mule-drawn wagon and carriage drives are also popular tourist activities. If you visit Sapelo Island, a Georgia state park, Maurice Bailey will take you on a mule wagon ride around the island to visit the lighthouse, old slave quarters, and a small historic church built of oyster-shell cement.

New Orleans and Savannah are two other Southern tourist destinations that offer mule-drawn carriage drives, carrying tourists back through time to view historic sites. The rides are spiced with true and not-so-true stories about the Old South. Evening rides often include ghost stories.

Military Service

In recent years mules have been called back into military duty. They are used to transport personnel and equipment in harsh landscapes, like the deserts and mountains of the Middle East and tropical jungle locations. Mules and other pack animals were used in Haiti in 1994 and have been used in Afghanistan since 2001.

The United States Army's John F. Kennedy Special Warfare Center and School at Fort Bragg, North Carolina, issued a 225-page field manual titled *Special Forces Use of Pack Animals* in 2004. Its introduction explains that the manual was written to fill a need that had not been used for decades. "It captures some of the expertise and techniques that have been lost in the United States (U.S.) Army over the last 50 years." The publication covers selection, care, and training of various pack animals, including the mule, in addition to military operations and maneuvers.

The manual's description of the mule includes all the characteristics civilian mule owners appreciate: "Intelligence, agility, and stamina. These qualities make mules excellent pack animals. Unlike horses, which carry about 65 percent of their weight on their front legs, mules carry 55 percent on their front legs. This trait makes them very well balanced and surefooted in rugged terrain."

Army Special Forces from Fort Bragg in Fayetteville, North Carolina, learn the proper way to pack a mule.   Photo by Shannon Hoffman

The description goes on to say, "Mules are intelligent and possess a strong sense of self-preservation. A packer cannot make a mule do something if the mule thinks it will get hurt, no matter how much persuasion is used. Therefore, many people confuse this trait with stubbornness."

With all the high-tech resources available, the mule is still doing its part in serving our country. There is something downright comforting about that.

Forestry Service

The Forest Service has used pack animals since the beginning of the twentieth century. In those early days, a ranger had to build his own cabin, furnish his own mule, and feed it out of his $75 per month salary. If the feed bill ran over that amount, the Forest Service sometimes reimbursed the expense.

Today the USDA Forest Service has two full regional mule pack strings, the Rocky Mountain pack and the Northern Region pack, and numerous smaller strings that are used to reach remote areas of the 191 million acres of national forests in places machines cannot access. Among all the land management agencies, about 1,300 to 1,500 head of horses and mules are in service.

The Rocky Mountain Region Pack String, which serves forests in Colorado, eastern Wyoming, Nebraska, Kansas, and South Dakota, and the Northern Region Pack Train, which serves Montana, northern Idaho, North Dakota, and northwest South Dakota, have a three-fold mission: to carry out work projects; represent the Forest Service by making public appearances at events like horse expos, fairs, parades, rodeos, veterans' homes and schools; and conduct educational clinics, including leave-no-trace-behind workshops, horsemanship, and packing. The teams can go anywhere in the United States. The mules and equipment are hauled with two semi-tractors pulling twenty-seven-foot-long trailers.

Other regions also use mules, primarily for work projects. The mule trains pack in supplies, gear, and crews to maintain trails and to build bridges, each carrying about two hundred pounds. Mules are used to carry in sand, gravel, and lumber, and even fish to restock streams. They also carry out junk, including airplanes, cars, and other scrap that detracts from the natural beauty of the wilderness. Large items like airplanes are cut with torches into manageable pieces.

When constructing a cable suspension footbridge at Rattlesnake Creek, Montana, the rolls of steel cable were too heavy for one mule. Several mules carried the cable, which was strung from mule to mule. It was very slow going for about twenty-five miles.

Rocky Mountain Region Pack String lead packer Glen Ryan says, "We pack out a lot of garbage."

Besides the usual trash left by trail users, some of the "garbage" found in national parks and forests is marijuana. The illegal pot farmers raise the weed in remote areas, where they pack it in as seedlings in small flowerpots. When the Forestry personnel find the plants, they pack them back out and destroy them. Ranger Ryan said on one occasion one of his mules ate a plant while his back was turned. He noticed no ill effects on the mule.

Ranger Ryan prefers buying his stock as three- or four-year-olds. He usually buys mules from private sources and dealers. If he gets one that doesn't work out, the seller will exchange it for another. One mule liked Ryan's company so much Ryan couldn't keep it out of his office. "I'm not stupid," he said, "I shut the door. But that mule just banged on the door with his foot, asking to come in." The gregarious mule was transferred to another district because it wasn't big enough to handle the job.

"Some of our mules are in their twenties. I keep them as long as I can. As long as they can do the work," he said.

Ryan says his mules are nice, quiet mules that behave well in crowds, as well as on wilderness trails. When they make public appearances, he never knows when a mother might roll a baby in a carriage up close to pet the mule, not realizing the danger that could be involved. His mules have to take those kinds of situations in stride.

"I am pretty proud of these guys," Ryan says of his mule string.

Logging

Mules and horses in logging operations are known to have less impact on the environment than heavy equipment. They can be used to do selective logging on small tracts of land and are more economical than machines. Most loggers who use mules also find that working with living creatures is an advantage over machines for the comradeship, as well as knowing their work is better for the environment.

Jason and Aaron Deschu of Brinktown, Missouri, own Triangle D Mule Logging. The brothers work with their mule team, Belle and Sugar, specializing in working small tracts of land that the big companies do not find profitable. Jason and Aaron grew up in St. Louis with little exposure to horses or mules, except through some short rides with the Boy Scouts and with their mother who enjoyed horses. The brothers learned their mule-skinner skills while working for the National Forest Service as young men in Wyoming. Jason has a forestry degree from Missouri State and Aaron has a degree in wildlife management. It was apparent they both planned to work outdoors. They found their niche in the logging industry.

Aaron said, "The Forest Service is where both of us got our knowledge. We have been packing mules and riding horses on multiday work trips into the wildernesses of western Wyoming for the last seven years."

When asked the pros and cons of using mules for their work, Aaron answered, "The pros of working with mules in my opinion are that they seem to be very intelligent animals, excited to have a job to do, very hardy, and easy keepers. They don't cost thousands to keep operating, and they don't tear up the ground like some of the heavier equipment does.

"The whole process it is quite enjoyable—to go out and log with a living animal doing the work of a machine; it's like working with a friend. For me one of the best feelings I get from working Sugar and Belle in the woods is how responsive they are, how intent they are on the work they're doing. We drive them down a tight path through the woods and ask them to perform some very tight maneuvers to position the logging cart, so we can snake the logs up out of the woods. They get excited and anticipate when it's time to pull. As the pitch of the winch changes under the load, they get antsy, waiting for my command to let them pull. It is just pure enjoyment to work with an animal that just truly enjoys working."

In all of the various workplaces where mules are used, they are lauded for their intelligence, agility, stamina, and personality. Those who are fortunate enough to work alongside a mule find the companionship priceless as well.

CHAPTER SEVEN

Pleasure Mules

Latest estimates indicate there are about 275,000 mules in American today. Pleasure riding and driving mules have become increasingly popular and account for most of that number. Perhaps their reputation for being hardy animals has led to this resurgence in the mule population, or maybe folks appreciate the heritage they represent. Many trail riders prefer mules over horses for their even temperament and sure-footedness. Some pleasure mule owners say they appreciate the animal's sense of humor.

Carolina Mule Association members on a pack trip in the Smoky Mountains, North Carolina.   Photo by Shannon Hoffman

James Lamm bought Rocky because of his personality and loud coloring.

James Lamm of Wake Forest, North Carolina, bought Rocky because of his personality and loud Appaloosa coloring. James says Rocky is a big ham, and he fell in love with him at first sight.

James has taught Rocky more than fifty tricks that they perform at shows and horse expos and for many civic and youth groups. James entered Rocky in the American Horse Idol Contest in Raleigh, North Carolina, in August 2007 and won the state's contest. He then went on to win the national contest, causing the organizers to change the name of the contest to America's Ultimate Equine Partner. They did not foresee a mule entering—and winning—the contest.

James rides Rocky through trail obstacle courses without a bridle or anything physical to guide the mule. He side passes, backs, and then walks onto a teeter-totter bridge. Rocky places his feet carefully on the bridge until it is perfectly balanced, with neither end touching the ground, a perfect example of a mule's intelligence and sure-footedness. James has been known to compete with Rocky in open show trail classes without using a bridle. When asked how

Rocky, on a teeter-totter bridge, exhibits a mule's uncanny sense of balance.

judges react to him showing without the bridle, James said, "Some of them think I am showing off."

Rocky jumps at liberty, fetches, bows, smiles, answers questions with a nod yes or no, and for a grand finale jumps into the bed of James's pickup truck, waits for the cue, and turns around and jumps out. He does most of his tricks either at liberty or under saddle with James aboard.

James said folks told him mules were hard to teach, so he was determined to prove them wrong. His secret is to never let Rocky know he is being trained. He says, "It has to be fun for Rocky, and I have to know when he has had enough for the day."

James, like many mule owners across the country, also enjoys trail riding. "I don't get to go as often as I'd like to," James says. That is because he stays so busy "showing off."

Not all mule-human relationships start out on the right foot. Just ask Sylvia Shannon, of Philadelphia, Mississippi. She has trained horses and thought she "had the training stuff under control." That was before she got her first mule.

She'd heard that once you rode a mule, there'd be no going back to horses. She decided a gaited molly would be the right mule for her, but that mule wasn't available at the time, and she instead bought a weanling john mule. She'd handled him in the pasture with his dam and all seemed to be going right, but when she got him in his stall and he caught sight of her horses, he commenced to have a little meltdown, braying and kicking. Sylvia hollered back. Her little mule turned his butt to her and started kicking with both hind feet in rapid succession, and then twice more. The mule didn't make contact with Sylvia, but she said it took almost a week before she dared approach her mule in the stall again. But she did succeed, at first with the stall door between them, in teaching the mule to allow her to halter him and to always turn and face her when she came to the door.

That's when Sylvia began to look for help through a mule forum on the Internet. She ended up selling the john mule. With more knowledge and experience and a borrowed mule, she continued to learn. Sylvia says mules are smarter than horses; they seem to have more reasoning power. The challenge in training a mule is you can't force them. The mule thinks about what's going on. If you pressure him he will balk, or perhaps "kick the living daylights out of you. If they don't see the need to do something, they're not going to do it."

Sylvia now has a yearling gaited molly mule. A gaited mule travels in a smooth four-beat gait. "Everything you've ever heard, good and bad, about mules is exhibited by this little molly. I think she'll be my dream mule if I can ever get her to bond to me." Right now Sylvia's molly mule, named Murray, has attached herself to a mare in the pasture and tries to leave with her every time Sylvia takes the mare out. Sylvia is up to the challenge of gaining Murray's trust and she is looking forward to the end result, a mule that is strongly bonded with her.

Deborah Cox and her husband own Upward Game Preserve in Montour Falls, New York. She has worked with horses many years, and six years ago she bought a mule. Remember Yahoo, the mule bought from a car dealer who claimed his young son rode the mule regularly? It turned out that the mule was a bucker. Deborah discovered this trait on her first ride. Here's her humorous story about why she gave the mule his name.

"He took off, bolted across an open field at a gallop, bucking. He was shocked at the far end of the field that I was still in the saddle. During the bolting, bucking, suicide gallop, I found my sense of humor—there was nothing else to do—and I said out loud, 'Yahoo!' Thus his new name."

That wasn't the only time Yahoo tried to unseat Deborah, and he was pretty creative at times. He'd spin around and even jump into holes front feet first, causing the saddle to slip up his neck. Deborah solved that trick by adding a breeching. "It has metal hearts on it decorating his hindquarters," Deborah said.

Deborah proceeded to take Yahoo back to the beginning in his training. She describes her experience working with Yahoo as "the summer of the mule." Finding time in her busy schedule as assistant dean in the College of Engineering at Cornell University, she worked Yahoo in the round pen. She started with voice cues, practiced Parelli Games ™ with him—a series of ground exercises—and she got tough when he misbehaved. After about a month of groundwork, she saddled him in her dressage saddle and rode him in the round pen. After that went well, she put him back in his Western tack and they hit the trails. Deborah says, "He has turned into a respectable trail mount."

While out riding one day, Deborah received a call on her cell phone. The ring tone spooked Yahoo, so when she got back to the barn she decided to expose him to the various tones. "I started playing them for him, and all of a sudden he rammed the phone with his nose. It flew out of my hand onto the ground."

When Deborah picked up the phone, she heard a man's voice say, "Hello, hello?" She quickly apologized and hung the phone up. Immediately the phone rang again and she answered it. The voice at the other end said, "Ma'am, this is the 911 operator; you just dialed us and we want to make sure you are okay." Deborah explained to the operator her mule had dialed the number by mistake. "I almost died of embarrassment. I am sure the operator thought I was a whack job.

"You are never finished with a mule," Deborah comments. "The minute you think they are polished, they out-think you." Deborah's goal is for Yahoo to be beginner safe. She says he is a point-and-go mule. "He goes wherever you point him: through water, up steep banks, down ravines." He is almost where she wants him, especially when ridden in company, but she says he still can be a challenge when ridden alone.

Deborah affirms that she and Yahoo have a special bond, "I consider him a pleasure mule and now one of my best friends."

Janeen Lemke has five pleasure mules that she and her sons, Peter and Aaron, enjoy trail riding, showing, and driving. She has owned mules for over fourteen years and horses for forty-three years. When asked how mules are different from horses, she points out that in all the years she's had mules, unlike with her horses, she has never had the vet out for sick or injured mules. "They are very hardy and into self-preservation," she says.

She has also found mules to be extremely versatile and intelligent. "Once they have learned something, they never forget it. This can be used to your advantage, or it can be frustrating if they've been taught the wrong thing," she says. Janeen explains that when you are training a mule, you can stop anywhere

Peter Lemke rides Tuxedo in a root beer race.   Photo courtesy of Janeen Lemke

in his training and go for weeks, months, or a year and pick up right where you left off. With a horse, the horse is often rusty and needs a few refresher courses. She says with a mule, it is as if you just worked with it the day before.

Another characteristic Janeen has come to appreciate about mules is how they will become bonded to a particular person. "It seems to have a 'crush' on that person," she says. "They will follow you around like a dog, hanging their head over the fence or gate, and looking very dreamy-eyed. It is really quite amusing."

We met Shannon Hoffman earlier; she owns three mules and a donkey. "I have several mules because they are like potato chips—you can't have just one!" She explains she got her first mule after donating her horse for a 4-H project. "Jake was not happy going camping. He was a good trail horse, but he wanted to sleep in," she said about her horse.

Shannon Hoffman and her three mules, Shiloh, Seven, and Sadie Mae.

Sadie Mae.

Shannon had been around some mules on trail rides and liked what she observed. She wanted a mount that was steady and strong and would do well camping out on the trails. She says each of her mules has a purpose.

"Seven is my show/try anything mule. He keeps me on my toes, which in turn keeps me safe." Shannon bought her second mule, Shiloh, to learn how to drive and to enjoy it. She has also used Shiloh to start other mules driving and to teach people how to drive. Sadie Mae is the mule that friends who want to go on trips with Shannon can ride safely. Sadie Mae also serves as a pack mule on some of Shannon's trips. Chester, the donkey, is Shiloh's companion when Shannon takes the other two mules on trips.

Sadie Mae even served as an ambulance on one occasion. Shannon had taken Sadie Mae on an overnight ride at Blowing Rock, North Carolina. On the second day of the ride, Shannon and a group of friends took a trail to an overlook point. Coming back down the trail, they met another group of riders, one of whom had fallen and severely injured her ankle. Her friends were trying to walk her out, but it was three more miles to the parking area. Shannon said, "Because Sadie is so steady and doesn't mind people all over her and she is so smooth to ride, we got several men to help the young lady onto Sadie. I led her back to the parking lot, where Sadie delivered the lady to her car so she could go to the hospital."

The following day Sadie's assistance was needed again, this time to tow her buddy Chester the donkey, who about halfway back from the ride decided he had had enough. Chester balked, refusing to go another step. "We used Sadie to drag him along for a while until he decided to go. What a great mule," Shannon says of her Sadie Mae. "Not much fazes her, so we can do just about anything."

When asked what it means to have a mule for a companion, Shannon summed it up like this: "A good mule that trusts you will do or try anything for you. They are like your best friend growing up and your best dog all combined. Mules make you grow as a person because you have to be good enough for them to accept and continue to trust you."

CHAPTER EIGHT

Mule Days

Mule Days festivals are held in several cities across the country, especially in the South, where mules played such an important role in agriculture, and in the West, where the mule is celebrated for transporting settlers during the westward movement. Each Mule Days event celebrates the mule its own way, but the common thread is to pay homage to the mule and have as much fun as humanly possible while doing it.

Bishop Mule Day's organizers in Bishop, California, claim they have the biggest of all mule festivals. The event has been held over Memorial Day weekend since 1969. Its Web site www.muledays.org describes the Bishop Mule Days as "part mule show, part test of skills, and part Wild West Show." The activities include fourteen mule shows with over seven hundred entries, steer roping and penning contests, concerts, dances, food, and arts and crafts. They also claim to have the longest non-motorized parade in the country.

Mule Days president Sondra Lozier says if there is one quote that sums up The Hells Canyon Mule Days in Enterprise, Oregon, it is, "We are more than you expect." It is a three-day event that has been held the Saturday after Labor Day since 1981.

Lozier explains that the community wanted to highlight the mule's role in settling Wallowa County and Hells Canyon. Mules were the mainstay of transportation during that time and are still used by many packers and guides, as well as the U.S. Forest Service.

She said, "They are just a wonderful animal, and oh so smart!"

Hells Canyon Mule Days offer a variety of contests, such as a packer's scramble, wild cow milking, and even a stick mule contest for the kids. Other

The Fast Ass Express.   Courtesy of Hell's Canyon Mule Days. Photo by Tim Peters

activities include the Cowboy Poetry Gathering, a quilt show, a jump-off challenge, and trail and packing workshops.

The Lion's Club in Calvary, Georgia, has sponsored Mule Days for thirty-
five years. The event is held the first Saturday of November and draws 60,000
to 90,000 people to the small town. In addition to the parade, mule show, and
plowing contests, events include a turkey shoot, flea market, and demonstra-
tions of old-time farming practices.

The Maury County Saddle and Bridle Club sponsors Mule Days in Columbia, Tennessee. The money from the festival is used to make improvements to
the county park and to support youth horse and mule clubs and various local
charities. They host mule shows, a parade, a mule auction, and a mule and donkey seminar. Don't miss the Liar's Contest and Checkers Tournament at the
Columbia Mule Days.

Mule Days in Benson, North Carolina, held the fourth weekend of September, may hold the record for the longest-running mule days. The Chamber
of Commerce first held the event in 1950. Organizers estimate around 70,000
people attend, quite a jump from their normal population of 4,000. Benson

Larry Walters and his mule team, Sis and Ernie, at the 2005 Hells Canyon Mule Days.

celebrates the mule because in its heyday the mule was the driving force of the town's economy; there were twelve mule dealer stables. The mule sales led to other businesses, like mule-drawn equipment and harness.

Benson Mule Days' parade lasts over two hours. Mule shows, rodeo, a pulling contest, mule race, team penning, and coon jumping are some of the most popular events. Coon jumping is a performance class where the mules jump in-hand rather than being ridden over hurdles. A beauty contest, golf tournament, music, dancing, and food round out the weekend that changes the small town to a boomtown.

Liz Wyatt, owner of Wyatt Ranch in Jacksonville, North Carolina, doesn't have a mule, but she hauled her horse to Benson. During Mule Days, hotels allow guests to park their trailers and set up portable pens for their mule or horse to stay. She rode on horseback to see the sights, which included mules, donkeys, and horses of all shapes, sizes, and colors decked out in everything from a halter and lead rope to the finest saddles and harnesses money can

About 70,000 people attend the Mule Days Festival each year in Benson, North Carolina.
Photo by Liz Wyatt

buy. Ox-drawn wagons, a man riding a steer, and a horse pulling a golf cart were a bit unusual even for Mule Days, but welcomed nevertheless. Liz said, "A mule-drawn wagon in the fast food line is usual. Even I have bought a Big Mac on horseback. All was well until she [the horse] decided to reach her head in through the window and take a whiff of french fries."

When asked to paint a picture of Benson's atmosphere, Liz said, "Imagine a town-wide carnival and all the things that go with it. Clothes vendors, funnel cake, gyros, Ferris wheels, parades, and traffic. Now, instead of strolling through the streets filled with people, imagine those people on horses, mules, donkeys, wagons, or the occasional golf cart."

According to a September 2006 article in Raleigh, North Carolina's *News and Observer,* the town of Benson has some rules for the 70,000 people who attend their Mule Days festivities. They include no cussing on the highway, no urinating in people's yards, no drinking on the streets, and no riding mules or horses on the streets after dark. These rules are intended to change the celebration's reputation for being a wild and crazy four days to one of good family entertainment.

Many will tell you it all depends on where you hang out and what you want to experience when you go to Mule Days. Jennifer Berry says Benson Mule Days is packed with people everywhere. "Nice people and families, kids eating junk food and visiting the rides at the carnival. Horses and mules are everywhere. Everyone acts like you've been friends forever. There is no such thing as a stranger there."

Jennifer certainly met one special friend at Mule Days in 2001. She wasn't even planning to go that year, but a friend invited her to come along and she relented. They arrived late and met some friends outside a popular Benson bar and grill called Lazy K's. Like an old Western movie, Lazy K's has a hitching rail in front of the building. Jennifer noticed a cowboy ride up, dismount, and hitch his horse to the rail. Chris Berry walked over and introduced himself to the group. The chemistry was working right from the beginning. Jennifer asked him if his horse rode double, and when he answered "Yes," they rode off into . . .

Mules on parade at Mule Days in Benson, North Carolina.   Photo by Liz Wyatt

Picking up the blue.

well, not the sunset—it was already nighttime. They headed toward one of the two arenas in town where many of the Mule Days events take place.

Along the way Chris asked Jennifer if she could make homemade biscuits. When she said "Yes," he asked Jennifer to marry him and laughed.

As they approached the arena, they came upon a mud hole. Chris's horse spooked and they both fell. "What a night," Jennifer says. "We've been together ever since then and were married in 2005." They now have two children and still own that horse that "threw them together." Chris and Jennifer go back every year to Benson Mule Days.

The Berrys' story isn't the only Benson Mule Days romance. Many Mule Days goers remember the cowboy wedding that took place in the middle of the rodeo arena one year. The bride in her wedding dress and groom in a Western style suit said their vows, and then the day's activities carried on.

So, whether you are looking for good, clean family entertainment, a love connection, a rip-roaring wild time, or to just celebrate the humble mule, a Mule Days someplace in the country has it all.

CHAPTER NINE

Mules in Competition

Mule shows are on the increase, and many open horse shows are including classes for mules. Mules can do everything a horse does, plus they have some unique events of their own. It is fun to win in any event, but mule owners feel a special satisfaction when they come out with the blue when showing their mule in a class full of horses.

Suzanne Lougee was first introduced to showing mules as a youth exhibitor. She'd been riding hunter jumper horses until that time. Now she shows her two mules, Mattie and Buckwheat, at open horse shows, as well as at mule shows all over the country.

"The first thing that really got me hooked was the incredible diversity that mules have. I was able to take one mule to a show and show halter, English performance, Western performance, driving, and gaming classes. Not only could my mule show in these different events, but it would ribbon in all classes and win in more than one division."

Suzanne's mule Buckwheat won the 2005 season high point award in the Novice Western Pleasure Horse Division in the Triangle Wide Horseman Association, a horse show circuit in central North Carolina. Buckwheat was the only mule shown in the association at that time, competing against some of North Carolina's top show horses. Suzanne says her competitors viewed her mule as inferior at first, but Buckwheat soon proved himself as a superior Western Pleasure mule. Suzanne and Buckwheat were able to educate people on the ability and diversity of mules.

Buckwheat is a dun, with distinctive zebra stripes on his legs and a stripe that runs down each shoulder. Suzanne has had some folks ask, "How did you get the stripes on that mule?" She tells them she had nothing to do with the

Kim Foushee rides End of the Drive Mr. Ike in a Western Pleasure class.

stripes and that many horses have the same markings, as do donkeys. But her husband likes to pull the questioner's leg sometimes by replying, "We spray paint them on before the show to attract the judge's attention." Suzanne says she is surprised at the number of people who say, "Really?" But she understands that while some questions seem silly, many people at the horse shows have never seen a mule before and just don't know much about them.

"I have lots of fun telling people about mules and why I like them," Suzanne says.

The North American Saddle Mule Association (NASMA) was established to preserve the records of sanctioned shows, as well as to organize and govern standard rules for mule and donkey competitions, promote the mule, and educate people about them. Affiliated groups across the country sponsor sanctioned mule shows. The Carolina Mule Association, which includes members from the Carolinas, Virginia, Georgia, and Tennessee, sponsors several shows a year, the largest one being at Denton Farm Park every fall. They offer halter, performance, trail, and timed game classes.

Most mule shows include halter and showmanship in-hand classes, performance classes, and light harness driving classes. Often mule shows will include coon jumping. The following divisions and classes are included in the NASMA rulebook. Local shows and 4-H might have different rules. Always check with the sponsoring organization to learn what rules govern their show.

In-Hand Classes

Halter classes are divided into age classes: weanlings, yearlings, two-year-olds, three-year-olds, four-year-olds, and over. Those classes can also be divided into john mules and molly mules. The four-year-olds and over may be split into two size divisions: 58.0 inches and under and 58.01 inches and over classes. Gaited halter mules have the same age, sex, and height categories, and there is a hunter-type halter division.

Sue King's Brayer Hill Farm in Boyd, Texas, is home to multiple mule and donkey champions. Also an officer of the North American Saddle Mule Association (NASMA), Sue explains that the judging criteria for mule halter classes are based on true form to function. She gives an example: "Stock mules are judged on their conformation and soundness to do ranch work." Conformation is how the mule is built, and it directly affects a mule's ability to perform. Halter classes divided by breed type are judged by the standards of conformation and movement for the breed of the dam of the mule. Gaited mules have their own classes because there are differences in their way of going, and draft mules are not shown with saddle mules.

King says, "Breed character is not important, although a dished face may suggest an Arab mom, or a big hip a Quarter Horse mom." Because the mule is sterile, it cannot pass its traits to offspring, therefore breed character does not enter highly into the judge's evaluation.

Shannon Hoffman, member of the North Carolina Horse Council, who shows her mules in open and sanctioned shows, agrees. "Just like in any halter class, the judge should be looking for conformation and quality. It seems the more like a horse, the better, and yes, people like longer ears. They say the longer-eared the mule, the better the mule. I am not sure about that, but I like the really long ears, too. I think overall quality and a strong top line would be more of a tiebreaker than longer ears. I would hope!

Showing in a halter class.

"We follow the same basic principles of balance and conformation as horse people do. All good conformation is form to function. Mules tend to be longer in the back and cow hocked, and finding one with a very good head and neck is harder."

Showmanship in-hand looks similar to a halter class. The exception is that the handler's ability to show the mule to its best advantage is being judged. The mule is merely a prop, and its conformation and soundness are not considered. Points are earned for grooming, standing the mule in a posed position according to its breed standard, and leading the mule, as well as the handler's appearance. The handler should be neat and clean and wearing appropriate attire depending on the class description (English or Western) or mule type in a combined class. Exhibitors' hair should be contained with a net and long hair should be worn in a braid or bun.

This class takes a great deal of preparation in training the mule to execute the routine and fitting the mule to its best health and appearance. The halter should fit the mule well and be clean, with any metal parts or decoration on the halter polished to a shine.

Mr. Ike and Julia Foushee.

Grooming Tips

Shannon Hoffman shows her Belgian-cross mules in Western, English, and trail classes. She shares some tips for grooming mules.

She says it begins with good nutrition. A balanced diet of concentrates with proper vitamins and minerals will produce a healthy looking mule with shiny feet and coat.

Elbow grease is the next step to a shiny mule. Groom with a curry comb or rubber grooming mitt "lots and often," Shannon advises.

Shannon uses Orvus Soap (Procter & Gamble), a mild detergent in a concentrated paste form that can be found in tack and farm supply stores, to wash her mules for a really deep clean. She clips her mules in the early spring, about two weeks before her first show, and again in late summer for the fall show season. Before clipping, she washes the mule and waits for it to dry completely. This makes clipping easier and is less wearing on the clipper blades. She clips the whiskers, around the nose and eyes, the ears, a four- to five-inch bridle path, the top of the tail, and—depending on how fuzzy these areas are—sometimes between the back legs, the back of the fetlock, and up the tendon.

Clipping a mule's mane.

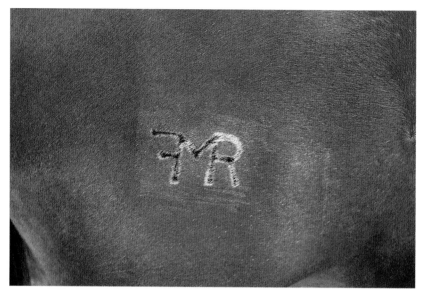

Clipping close over the brand gives a nice finishing touch.

Shannon uses full-size body clippers for the mane, tail, and legs and small battery-powered clippers for the ears and nose and touch-ups. She uses body clippers and clips the hair short, usually in a square, around any brands so that you can read the brand more easily.

Shannon says, "There is a clip called the Tennessee Clip. You clip three inches behind the throatlatch forward, getting the whole face. They do this at the Tennessee mule sales in January and February. Basically, it shows off the mule's throatlatch and head but still allows them to be turned out in cold weather."

Some mule owners like to clip the mule's tail according to old military tradition in cuts called the bell tail and the shave tail. The "bells" were used in the military to signify the mule's training: one bell meant the mule was broke to pack; two bells, broke to pack and drive; three bells, broke to pack, drive, and ride. A shaved tail warned the mule was new and not yet trained for duty.

For a nice foot, Shannon uses plumber's PVC glue on the bottom half of the outside of the hoof to close in the nail holes, which prevents rot and keeps the shoes on tight. It is permissible to use black hoof polish on mules with black feet or clear polish on light-colored or striped hooves.

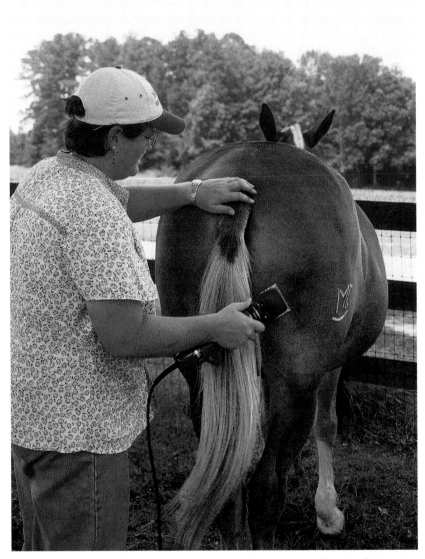

A shaved tail warned that the army mule was new and not yet trained for duty. Today it is simply a matter of style.

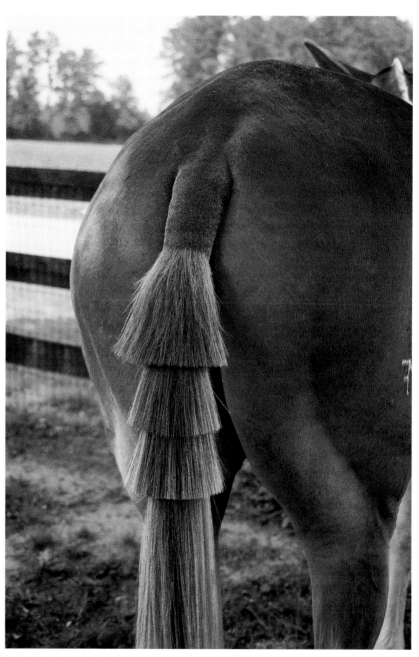

Bell tails identified what the army mule could do: one bell broke to pack, two bells broke to pack and drive, three bells broke to pack, drive, and ride.

For a finishing touch Shannon applies baby oil to the mule's muzzle, around the eyes, and in the ears.

Be sure you clean your tack and make sure that it fits properly. As for her apparel, when she rides in Western and specialty classes, Shannon likes to wear old-style Western wear like that worn by cowboys and muleteers in the early 1900s. She says, "Do not groom to perfection and then show in overalls!"

Performance Classes

Performance classes include Western Pleasure, Western riding, working cow horse, cutting, reining, English Pleasure, dressage, jumping, mulemanship (equitation), and trail. In large shows, there are separate classes for gaited mules. Gaited mules are from Tennessee Walking Horses, Racking Horses, or other smooth-gaited breeds, so-called for the four-beat smooth gait called a rack or running walk.

Shannon Hoffman works a trail class obstacle riding Shiloh.

A Trakehner-cross mule wins an English class.

Gaited mule.

Amy Finger of Simpsonville, South Carolina, bought her mule Absolutely Priceless, also known as Ada, to show in English and jumping classes. She has shown successfully in English under-saddle classes but is taking the jumping training slowly, since Ada is only five years old. She also shows in showmanship classes and tracks steers, which is riding behind the steer to keep it going forward, for her fiancé, who competes in team roping.

Amy keeps Ada body clipped when she is showing because she gets very hairy. "It is just easier to keep her clean for the shows, and she looks much better." Ada gets a trace clip in winter so she doesn't get a chill from sweating.

When asked what kind of reception Ada gets when they show in open shows against horses, Amy said, "When I first showed up at the open shows people asked me what I was doing there. Then when I won classes they were a bit upset. But now Ada has her own fan club."

The Great Mule and Donkey Celebration in Shelbyville, Tennessee, was Amy and Ada's first big show. Amy noticed a difference at the big mule show from horse shows, in that the mules did not act excitable before entering the arena. Amy says from her experience mules have a much different personality than horses.

Ada took being in the big-time show in stride, placing in all of her classes.

Specialty Classes

Coon jumping has an interesting history that began in the hunting field. Raccoon hunting has a long heritage, especially in the South, from the era when the fur of this common animal was a valuable commodity. Hunters brought along their mules to pack the furs out. The need to cross fences in the chase behind coon hounds was no problem, since the mule is a very talented jumper. The long-eared equine hybrid can easily clear a fence as high as its own back from a standstill. A wire fence was tricky; if the mule did not clear it, he could get a nasty cut. To protect his mule from that danger, the hunter simply threw his jacket over the wire fence, led his mule up to the fence and gave the cue, and the mule jumped over it. The hunter then retrieved his coat and climbed across the fence.

Human competitive nature being what it is and some mules being better jumpers than others, there was soon a contest of whose mule could jump higher. Today, at mule shows all over the country, mules that never met a coon hound or a raccoon are competing for championship ribbons by jumping hurdles inside show arenas.

Mules have their own style of jumping. Their hindquarters are well under the body to give a good spring to the take off. In contests there are no running starts. The mule is led into a twelve- or ten-foot square box marked either by ground poles or lime. The handler leads the mule up to the fence, and, keeping the lead rope in his hand, he stops and then cues the mule to jump. He may stand on either side of the mule. Ninety seconds are allowed from the time the mule enters the box until he jumps the hurdle. If the contestant inside the box does not clear the hurdle from a standstill in two tries within the time period, it is disqualified. The pole is raised two inches after each round. The last mule to clear the hurdle wins.

The mule may be saddled or bareback. If it is saddled, the stirrups must be tied over the saddle. In some contests, the mules compete in full pack gear. No tack adjustments or changes are allowed once the mule is led into the box. Bridles or halters may be used, with halters being the more common headgear. Chains over the nose or in the mouth are not allowed.

Training the mule for coon jumping can begin before it is trained for riding. Starting in a place that prevents the mule from running around the pole makes

Rocky, practicing his coon-jumping form.

the process easier. A barn aisle or a jumping aisle is ideal. To make the jumping aisle, fashion a chute from jump standards and poles that lead up to the hurdle. If using the barn aisle, be sure the pole goes all the way across the aisle. Pass the lead to a helper on the other side of the obstacle, lead the mule up to the jump, and cluck to him from behind his eye. If he refuses to go forward, rattle a plastic bag behind him. This will usually get him moving forward and over the hurdle.

James Lamm says when he trains a mule for coon jumping, he starts the mule at a height that is easy for it to jump. "I start at eighteen inches, and if he jumps this height I stay with it until I am sure he knows I want him to jump and he is happy doing it. Then, I start raising the pole four inches at a time." James tries to judge the mule's comfort level and does not push him beyond it. When the mule fails to clear a jump, James is quick to lower it a level and start again. "I never let him finish for the day not clearing the jump, no matter how far down I have to lower it for him to end the day on a good note and clear the jump."

Costume is a specialty class at many mule shows and is very popular with the spectators as well as the showmen. North American Saddle Mule Association (NASMA) rules dictate that entries be in a costume that is authentic, showing animals as they are or were outfitted in any country, or representing a character in a book or artwork, or an occupation or sport in history or the present time. The entry must provide a descriptive narrative with optional music to the show committee before the class so it can be read during their one-minute performance. The class is judged for originality, authenticity, and spectator appeal.

Contestants have a lot of fun creating their mule's costumes, and the class is also fun for the spectators. Shannon Hoffman, who earlier explained mule grooming, remembers showing her mule Seven in costume as a Mexican mule. Mexican mules were a small type of mule raised in Mexico. She bought a big sombrero and yards of fabric in a bandana print. She tied the over-sized bandana around his neck so it hung almost to his knees, cut some ear-holes in the sombrero, and put it on Seven, making the costume a play on words.

Shannon says, "Seven loves to wear a hat with his ears sticking out. It is funny how he likes to wear a hat. People look at him, and I think he knows he is special." Seven did not win the class, but that did not diminish everyone's fun, including Seven's.

Free-style reining is another specialty class offered at large mule shows. In this class, typical reining maneuvers are done to music. The entrant picks the music with the approval of the show management. The entrant may be in costume, but this is not required. Required maneuvers are four spins to the right and four to the left, three stops, and lead changes in both directions. Rollbacks, backups, and speed maneuvers can be added and may affect the score. A four-minute time limit from the beginning of the music or introduction ends when the music stops.

Dressage is a highly disciplined form of riding in which a prescribed pattern is ridden to show the mule's suppleness, willingness, and quiet response to the rider's cues. When dressage is offered at a mule show, it is normally judged under the most current United States Equestrian Federation (USEF) rules.

Dressage offers several riding levels for mules in various stages of training, beginning with training level tests that call for simple transitions, changes of direction, and bending. In the higher level tests, mules are required to execute more complicated movements such as the half-pass, pirouette—a pivot on the inside hind foot—flying lead changes, and two of the most difficult movements, the passage and piaffe. In the passage, the mule performs a highly cadenced trot with a moment of suspension, where one diagonal pair of legs is on the ground and the other pair is elevated. A piaffe is also done at a trot, but the mule does not move forward—it trots in place.

Snigging is a timed event in which the mule is in harness, with the traces attached to a singletree that is hooked to a log. The handler guides the mule pulling the log in a serpentine pattern through a series of cones and back again to the start/finish line. The object is to finish the course in the shortest time without the mule or driver stepping on or over the cones, or the log disturbing any cones. There is a time penalty for each cone that is disturbed in any way. Going off pattern is cause for disqualification. No whips are allowed, but the handler may use his voice or moderate slapping of the reins to encourage the mule.

This class duplicates work done with mules in the forestry industry years ago. The mules had to pull logs out of the woods and be able to maneuver around trees and rocks without getting hung up on anything. The cones in the class represent trees.

Driving Classes

Various driving classes are also offered at mule shows. The foremost consideration is that the mule be safely harnessed to the vehicle. The only time two people are allowed in the vehicle is when two or more mules are hitched to the vehicle or when a junior exhibitor is showing. Even then, any assistance by the second person is cause for disqualification.

Appointments include a whip. The lash on the whip must be long enough to reach the shoulder of the mule farthest from the driver. No one may handle the reins, brake, or whip but the driver, nor can drivers be changed unless called for in the class description.

NASMA rules emphasize that the harness fit properly and be adjusted for the comfort of the mule. The bridle should fit snugly to prevent it catching on parts of the harness or vehicle. A throatlatch and noseband are required. Metal fittings should match and be secure.

In choosing between black or brown harness, keep in mind that black is correct for painted vehicles and natural stained wooden vehicles that are trimmed with black, whereas brown is correct if the natural wooden vehicle is trimmed with brown. Use a breast collar with a light vehicle and a full collar for pulling a heavy carriage or wagon.

When exhibiting in a driving class, one should consider the overall picture when choosing the vehicle. It should give a pleasing and balanced appearance in accordance with the size and type of mule and its way of going. The vehicle should be in good repair, painted or stained as appropriate, and be in keeping with the rules.

Yelling, whistling, or otherwise using the voice in excess can be penalized by the judge. Clucks and voice commands in a normal tone are permitted. As in any class, the showman should be able to control his or her animals with the least obvious cues possible. Conservative modern clothes, Western or English, are proper attire for driving classes. Women wearing a skirt should use a lap apron. Hats, long sleeves, and gloves are required.

The mules must be sound, showing no sign of lameness, shortness of wind, or visual impairment. Showmen should be sure their mules are appropriately shod for driving. All equipment must fit correctly and the harness type be appropriate to the class.

Pleasure driving working classes are judged based on the overall appearance of a pleasant drive that one might take on a Sunday afternoon in the countryside. The mule should show alertness, quality gaits, smooth transitions, and good manners. The class is scored 70 percent on performance, 20 percent on condition and fit of the harness and vehicle, and 10 percent on neatness of the turnout. The mules are shown in both directions of the ring at a walk, trot, park trot, and road trot. They will also be expected to stand quietly when asked, and to back. They may be required to do a figure eight.

Pleasure driving is judged 40 percent on performance, manners, and way of going, 30 percent on condition, fit, and appropriate harness and vehicle, and

Bonnie Croft conditions her mule for cross-country marathon driving classes.

30 percent on the turnout. The class routine is the same as in working pleasure driving.

Reinsmanship is similar to equitation in riding classes. It is judged 75 percent on the handler's ability and 25 percent on the condition and turnout of the harness and vehicle. The class routine includes showing at a walk, trot, park trot, and road trot in both directions of the ring, and competitors are also expected to stop, stand quietly, and to back. They may also be asked to execute a figure eight.

Obstacle driving classes require the mules be driven through an obstacle course. In this class, tie-downs and overchecks are prohibited. Each obstacle has a point value. The judge wants to see the mules negotiate the course smoothly without disturbing the obstacles. The mule should be alert and responsive to the driver's commands. There are six to eight obstacles. Four kinds of obstacle are mandatory: the back-through, box, serpentine, and straight-and-narrow, which is a set of parallel poles one foot apart and at least twenty-five feet long; the driver must keep one wheel between the poles for the entire length of the poles. No live animals or animal hides may be used and the driver may not dismount.

Double Jeopardy and Gamblers Choice are both timed driving classes. In Double Jeopardy, each vehicle has two drivers. The first driver negotiates the mule and vehicle through an obstacle course from start to finish, then hands the reins to the second driver, who drives the course in reverse order, finish to starting line. There is a prescribed time limit; if the team exceeds it they are penalized five seconds. Five-second penalties are also given if the team knocks over or dislodges an obstacle and for each time the mule breaks gait.

In Gamblers Choice, a course is set up and the obstacles are given a point value. The driver can choose his or her own path through chosen obstacles, gambling on earning the most points for successfully finishing the course within a two-minute time limit.

Since there may be some differences from one show to another, before entering one, find out what rules will govern the show. For example, the Carolina Mule Association uses the NASMA rulebook for the coon jump and other mule-specific classes, but they refer to the American Quarter Horse and North Carolina Open Horse Show rules for anything not covered in the NASMA rulebook. They also sponsor the World Championship Coon Jump. NASMA provides a download of their rulebook at their Web site http://nasma .net/official_20072009.htm.

Endurance Racing and Competitive Trail Riding

Given their history for cross-country trekking success, it seems natural a mule would be a likely candidate for endurance racing. They have made their mark in the sport; in 1976, two mules won a 3,200-mile endurance race from Frankfort, New York, across the U.S. to Sacramento, California. Each entry included two mounts to be alternately ridden and packed. Virl Norton entered with his Thoroughbred and Mammoth jack crosses Lord Fauntleroy and Lady Eloise. Norton and his mules beat the second-place winner, an Arabian, by nine hours and seventeen minutes, for a purse of $2,500.

The winner of an endurance race is the animal that finishes the course in the shortest time, whereas competitive riding is not a race but a contest, where a prescribed course must be run within a predetermined time limit.

Negotiating a trail obstacle.

Winners of a competitive trail ride are judged on soundness, manners, condition, and how obstacles are negotiated on the course. There are usually two judges; one judge must be a veterinarian. Riders lose points for being under or over the time limit. Historically, the Arabian horse has held reign in endurance and competitive trail riding. So, why not combine the two? Cindy Ross is a member of the Eastern Competitive Trail Riding Association, and she rides her Arab-cross mule, Ruby, in both competitive rides and endurance races.

Ruby is her second mule. She said, "My first mule was out of a Quarter Horse mare. She had no desire to do endurance. She would go all day, just not at any great speed. My present mule is out of an Arabian mare. She has the spark and physical ability that my first mule did not."

Cindy bought Ruby in May 2007. She put Ruby on a conditioning program, taking it slow and easy. She entered Ruby in two limited distance rides and two competitive trail rides. They placed in two races and won a race, taking first in the thirty-five-mile Hot Toddy Hustle I in Orland, Maine.

Bonnie Croft's favorite competition is the marathon, a driving event in which contestants drive a five-mile cross-country course. They are given a specific time to finish, like in a competitive trail ride. You lose points for being under or over the time limit. The course includes water, bridges, hills, fields, and roads. Bonnie says she likes this event because "all equines are equal."

NASMA also sanctions a Versatility Trail Program that promotes the recreational trail riding of saddle mules. Participating riders keep a log of the hours spent trail riding and turn it into NASMA. When the log is verified, the riders are awarded patches, ranging from fifty accumulated miles up to a two-thousand-mile patch.

Pulling Contests

Mule pulling is an elimination contest of strength. Two-mule teams pull a sled with 1,000-pound weights. More weight is added after each round. Mule teams can compete with draft horses or in contests specifically for mules. Mules are given either a time limit or a distance they must pull the load. Rules vary depending on the location of the contest. In many contests teams are given three tries to pull 27.5 feet. Some rules specify the distance to be pulled in one of three tries; other rules tally the distance of all three goes.

Some contests use a dynamometer, a machine that measures horsepower, invented in the 1920s by researchers at the Iowa State University in Ames, Iowa. When the mule pulls against the collar, preset weights are lifted, an oil valve is released, and oil flows through the machine. When the team stops pulling, the weights drop and close the valve. The resistance weight is increased until the winning team pulls 27.5 feet at the maximum preset weight on the dynamometer. The starting weight varies from pull to pull, depending on what kind of ground they are on and what kind of boat is used.

Most contests have two team divisions, lightweight and heavyweight. Teams weighing under 3,400 pounds are lightweights and those weighing 3,400 pounds and over are heavyweights. Some mule pulls have classes for individual pullers.

Hookers are assistants who hook the team to the sled or dynamometer. Hookers are then required to stand back without encouraging the team or speaking to the driver in any way. This can be a risky job, since the mules are anxious to begin pulling; if a hooker doesn't get out of the way fast, he can get caught between the team and the sled.

CHAPTER TEN

Breeding and Foal Care

In speaking of breeding in relation to mules, we are not talking about breeding mules to produce mules. Although in very rare instances female mules have produced offspring, for all practical purposes the mule is sterile. As was mentioned earlier, the horse and the donkey do not have matching pairs of chromosomes. All members of a species have the same number of chromosomes in a cell. The horse has sixty-four and the donkey sixty-two, the mule inherits thirty-two from the horse parent and thirty-one from the donkey, giving it sixty-three, an odd number of chromosomes that cannot evenly divide and so will not match up to produce offspring. So when we speak of breeding mules, we mean the mating of horse and donkey to produce a mule.

Even though they are sterile, female mules have estrus cycles. All reproductive organs and hormones are intact; female mules and hinnies have even been used as surrogate mothers for embryo transfer.

As previously mentioned, male mules produce testosterone but not sperm. They will exhibit stallion behavior if not gelded, so it is best to geld them. There are no known instances of a male mule being fertile.

As in all equine breeding programs, the key to success is choosing the very best sire and dam possible. An offspring cannot be better than the genetic codes contributed by its parents. There are a great many variables in bringing the two species, horse and donkey, together, so there must be a clear understanding of what the breeder wants from the offspring. Does the breeder want a saddle mule, work mule, or driving mule? If miniature mules are the goal, then finding the best miniature horses and miniature donkeys is the top criterion. It is not enough that they just be small; the parents must have good conformation and disposition in order to pass those traits to the foals. The same goes for breeding the draft mule and saddle mule.

Research mule journals and mule associations' membership lists and visit farms and mule shows. These are valid ways to find reputable breeders with good stock. One of the best ways to judge whether a jack produces quality mules is to look at offspring by that particular jack. If you plan to buy a jack and start your own program, be sure to find out if he has bred mares before. Some jacks will refuse to service mares, especially those jacks that have only bred female donkeys.

Today's high tech world offers more options. Shopping online for a sire widens the horizons. Frozen semen for artificial insemination can be shipped from anywhere in the world. Most horse vets are equipped to handle the insemination if the breeder does not have the knowledge and equipment required.

The jack is said to contribute long ears, voice, sure-footedness, and hardiness. The mare gives the mule a more horse-like head and eye shape, size, conformation, and disposition.

The mare should have excellent conformation, with a prominent wither. This feature is important, since the donkey lacks this attribute, and good withers are necessary to hold a saddle in place. This is particularly important if the mule will be a pack animal. The mare should have a pleasing head and long neck. Avoid mares with such flaws as a roman nose, long back, crooked legs, or unbalanced build. These flaws are very likely to appear in the mule. You want a nice blend of the two animals, with neither dominating the other. While there are no guarantees even with the best sire and dam, it certainly increases the likelihood of producing a high-quality mule when you choose high-quality parents.

Breeding for color should be the least consideration; never choose a mate for color over good conformation and disposition. Size is important, but this goal is not without its problems. Miniature horses and donkeys can have some genetic problems due to dwarfism in the small breeds. Be sure neither mate exhibits any dwarf characteristics, which can range from minimal to severe, including short legs with an oversized head and body, retracted tendons, club feet, an undershot jaw or parrot mouth, a dished face and bulging forehead, and mental retardation. A minimal dwarf usually is one with short legs, poorly aligned jaw, or other minor physical deformity.

Introducing the Jack and Mare

One of the challenges of breeding the jack and mare is that often the jack is reluctant to service a mare. Even George Washington's early breeding experiments ran into this problem, when Royal Gift, the first jack he received from the King of Spain, turned up its nose at Washington's mares. Only after a second jack was brought to Mount Vernon and Royal Gift had some competition were Washington's attempts at mule production successful.

Today's breeders often run into this problem, particularly if the jack has covered female donkeys prior to being introduced to mares. They advise introducing novice jacks to mares before they are allowed to breed jennets.

The tables can also be turned, when the mare rejects the jack. Susan Morgan, who runs a miniature equine rescue on her Painted Promise Ranch in Wittmann, Arizona, learned early on that her miniature mares did not care for her little jack. After attempting to pasture breed two of her mares and having them gang up on the poor jack and kick him, she had better results giving him one mare at a time. Even then she had to muzzle the jack, since he got carried away biting the mare's neck. Muzzling solved the problem, and Susan got her first miniature mule foal.

Vickie and James Rauh, owners of Diamondback Mules in Mooreland, Oklahoma, also found that not all of their mares liked jacks. They have selected mares from show and working bloodlines so their mules would have the genetic makeup buyers are seeking. Vickie says she has one beautiful foundation Quarter Horse that simply refuses the attention of the jack. Vickie believes future artificial insemination will solve the problem.

Care of the Pregnant Mare

The pregnant mare's care includes conditioning, good nutrition, and all of the preventive care that should be offered any equine. It is especially important that she be up to date on all vaccinations and booster injections. These antibodies will be passed on to the foal when it drinks the mare's colostrum immediately after birth. Parasite control in the pregnant mare is also very important to maximize the health of both the mare and the fetus.

Jack, Diamondback Cowboy, is offered at stud to mares and jennets at James and Vickie Rauh's Diamondback Mules, Mooreland, Oklahoma.
Photo courtesy of Vickie Rauh

Exercise is important in maintaining all-around good health for the mare. Light riding and plenty of turnout space for free exercise will benefit the mare during her pregnancy.

Feeding the pregnant mare does not change dramatically until the last trimester of pregnancy. At this time the amount of food may need to increase, and a calcium/phosphorous supplement may be needed. After the foal is born, increase the mare's protein ration to 16 percent for as long as she is nursing the foal.

A clean living environment is extremely necessary to the mare and foal's well being. The ideal situation is a well-managed pasture. In fact, a pasture is the best place for a mare to give birth. When this is not possible and the mare is kept in a paddock or stall, those quarters should be cleaned daily.

Parturition

As the foaling date approaches, the mare owner or breeding manager will look for certain signs to warn of the impending birth. Normally the first sign her time is getting near is the filling out of the udder. This usually occurs two to six weeks before birth. Then about one week before birth, the muscles of the croup area become very relaxed. The teats fill out and wax-like beads form on the tips about two to four days before birth.

As the time draws nearer, the mare will become restless. She may seem colicky and look at her side, lie down and get back up, and urinate frequently. If in a stall, she will walk in circles, repeatedly lying down and getting back up.

In a normal birth the two front feet appear first, with the nose right behind them. The bottom of the hooves should be pointed down. Any deviation from this presentation should be cause for alarm, and the veterinarian should be called at once. Normal delivery should take no more than thirty minutes.

Miniature horses often have problems giving birth due to their size. They should be observed carefully when the time comes near for them to foal so a veterinarian can be called if there is trouble. A foal too big for the birth canal or a mal-positioned foal can cause dystocia (difficult birth), and delivery by C-section may be required.

Miniature mule foal is nursing.   Photo courtesy of Susan Morgan, Painted Promise Ranch

Draft horses are prone to retained placentas and giving birth to twins, as well as dystocia. If you are breeding a draft mare to a Mammoth jack, you might run into this problem. Work closely with your vet during the mare's pregnancy. Preparation and knowledge are the keys to producing a healthy mule. If you can find out the mare's previous breeding history, this information should also factor into the decision whether to breed this mare to a jack.

Gestation for the donkey carrying a donkey foal is twelve months, about one month longer than that of horses. The mare will likely carry the hybrid foal a few days longer than she would a horse foal. Follow the same veterinarian-recommended nutritional guidelines, vaccinations, and deworming program as you would if she was carrying a horse foal.

While some might expect the incidence of foal rejection to be high with mares that give birth to a mule, studies show this is not true. The mare is just as attentive to her mule baby as the mare that produces a horse.

Care of the Newborn Foal

Examine the foal and make sure the membranes are cleared from the foal's nostrils so it can breathe. Once you are sure the foal is breathing, leave it and the mare alone to rest. The resting time allows oxygen-carrying blood to transfer from the placenta to the foal before the umbilical cord breaks.

The umbilical cord should break naturally when the mare stands up. The placenta is usually expelled within two hours after the foal is born. If the placenta is not expelled within four hours, infection can occur and cause serious conditions such as founder, colic, or septicemia. In this case, veterinarian care is vital. Once the placenta has been expelled, examine it to be sure it is intact, since any part of it left inside the mare can lead to infectious complications.

The first milk, or colostrum, contains antibodies important to building the foal's immunity against diseases. Colostrum level is at its highest within the first twelve hours of birth. The newborn should be up nursing within the first hour to get full benefit from the antibodies in the colostrum. The foal cannot absorb these life-saving antibodies after it is twenty-four hours old.

It is wise to have a vet examine the foal to be sure it is breathing normally and that all is well with both foal and mare.

Navel ill, also called joint ill, shigellosis, or sleepy foal disease, is caused by a bacterial infection that enters the foal through the navel stump. It can also infect the foal through the placenta before birth. Symptoms include depression, fever, not nursing, and swollen joints. In most cases the foal will die. To prevent this condition it is important to soak the stump with iodine solution once the umbilical cord is broken. Good hygiene is an important preventive measure, so keep the stall clean and free of flies. If a mare has had a previous foal with navel ill, it is possible the present foal contracted the disease before birth and the mare should not be bred again.

It is important that the mare and foal be housed in a safe environment. The foaling stall should provide room for the mare to move around without stepping on the foal. Turnout paddocks or pastures should have adequate fencing and good footing and be free of obstacles that can cause injury to the mare or foal.

"Bunny," a healthy molly mule and her dam, Jessie. Owned by James and Vickie Rauh of Diamondback Mules, Mooreland, Oklahoma.   Photo courtesy of Vickie Rauh

Care should be taken that other horses do not cause the little mule to run excessively, since too much exercise and separation from its dam can cause stress. Worm the foal every two weeks until it is one year old and keep its environment clean.

Scours is a common type of diarrhea in foals that usually occurs when they are eight to twelve days old. It is caused by intestinal adjustment to digestion of food. It usually corrects itself in one or two days. If diarrhea lasts longer than forty-eight hours it can cause dehydration. Diarrhea may be caused by internal parasites, stress, or bacterial infection, which can be deadly.

Neonatal isorythrolysis (NI) is a condition that occurs rarely in horses but is found in 10 percent of mule foals. NI is an immunologic condition comparable to the Rh negative blood factor in humans. It happens when the jack and the mare have different blood types, which is likely in the mating of two different species. When the mare is pregnant, fetal cells can pass through the placenta into the mare's blood and meet up with the blood cells of a different type inherited by the foal from its sire. The mare's body produces antibodies against these cells that are not compatible to her own cells. The antibodies are then transferred to the foal when it drinks the first milk, or colostrum, and the foal's red blood cells are destroyed, leading to the death of the foal. Symptoms include depression, yawning, increased heart and respiratory rates, jaundice, and dark urine. The foal will go into a coma in the last stages, then die. Treatment includes blood transfusions and antibiotics. Success depends on how severely anemic the foal is and how quickly treatment is started.

It is possible to prevent NI by having the sire and dam tested before breeding to ensure their blood types are compatible. If not, they should not be bred. If incompatible sire and dam are bred, steps must be taken to make sure the foal does not nurse its mother for at least thirty-six hours. Muzzle the foal and allow it to stay with its mother. Colostrum from another mare should be provided during that time period. The mare should also be milked to remove the colostrum. The foal can nurse after thirty-six hours.

Vaccination and deworming programs should begin when the foal is four to six weeks old. Flu and rhino boosters should be given about six months later. Follow the advice of your veterinarian for a vaccination and deworming program.

Weaning the Foal

The mule foal can be weaned as early as four months old if it is eating well by then. The easiest way to wean the foal is to offer a buddy, whether another foal, a gentle old gelding, or even a goat. Separate the mare and foal so they cannot see or hear each other. Weaning usually only takes about a week or two. Some breeders use a gradual weaning method, separating the mare and foal with a sturdy fence. The foal can stand side by side with the mare but not nurse. Some foals cannot tolerate this and will try to jump the fence to get back to their dams. Older mule babies that have become very bonded to their dams sometimes become hysterical when separated from their dams. For this reason many mule breeders are careful to wean by four months, as long as the little mule is eating well and otherwise healthy.

A truckload of mule.

Resources

American Donkey & Mule Society
P.O. Box 1210
Lewisville, TX 75067
P: (972) 219-0781 | F: (972) 420-9980
E-mail: adms@juno.com
Web site: www.lovelongears.com

**American Gaited Mule
Association**
Bill Moore
PO Box 764
Shelbyville, TN 37160

American Mule Association
P.O. Box 1349
Yerington, NV 89447
E-mail: masmules@aol.com
Web site: www.jesmon.com/ama

American Mule Racing Association
PO Box 660651
Sacramento, CA 95866

American Mule Racing Association
Endurance Division
Box 177
North Fork, ID 83466

**Canadian Donkey & Mule
Association**
Jackie Dunham
Box 229
Hey Lakes, Canada T0B 1W0

Carolina Mule Association
3504 Lake Wheeler Road
Raleigh, NC 27603
E-mail: cmamule-mail@aol.com

DV Auction, Inc.
1200 Kelland Dr.
Norfolk, NE 68701
(402) 474-5557
www.dvauction.com

**International Zebra-Zorse-
Zonkey Association**
1672 Main St. East
PMB 454
Ramona, CA 92065

Mules n More Magazine
PO Box 460
Bland, Missouri 65014
(573) 646-3934

**North American Saddle Mule
Association**
PO Box 343
Boyd, Texas 76023
(940) 389-5608

Western Mule Magazine
PO Box 46
Marshfield, Missouri 65706
(417) 859-6853

Glossary

Anemic: Low red-blood-cell count

Antibiotics: Medication that can kill harmful organisms or bacteria

Antibodies: Immunizing agent in the body that fights disease

Artificial insemination: A method of breeding in which the semen is collected from the stallion or jack and injected into the uterus of the mare or jennet

Auction: A sale in which the mule is sold to the highest bidder

Azoturia, or Monday morning disease: A metabolic disorder in which large amounts of lactic acid accumulate in the muscles and destroy muscle cells, releasing myoglobin into the system. This causes muscle stiffness after exercise.

Breeching: A saddle accessory that fits across the mule's hips and prevents the saddle from slipping forward when riding downhill

Chestnut: A natural horny growth on the inside of the front legs just above the knees

Chromosome: The part of a cell that carries the genes. They come in pairs, one from each parent.

Coggins test: A blood test used to detect equine infectious anemia

Colostrum: A mare's first milk that contains antibodies, which provide the foal with immunity against many diseases

Concentrate: Food that is high in energy-producing carbohydrates

Conformation: Equine body structure and proportions

Crupper: A strap that fits around the top of the tail and attaches to the saddle to stabilize it on hills

Dam: The mother

Deworm: To administer a medication that kills internal parasites

Donkey: A member of the equine family originating in northern Africa

Dwarfism: To have characteristics of a dwarf, a small and usually deformed animal

Dynamometer: A machine that measures the weight a mule can pull

Dystocia: A difficult birth

Embryo transfer: Transferring a fertilized egg from one mare's uterus to another mare's uterus. The recipient mare is called a surrogate mare.

Equine Infectious Anemia (EIA): A viral disease that affects the immune system. Biting insects or contaminated needles transmit EIA.

Equine Polysaccharide Storage Myopathy (EPSM): A condition found in draft horses in which glycogen and glycogen-related compounds are stored in the muscles instead of being used as energy. This leads to various symptoms, including a stiff gait, muscle cramps, shivers, azoturia, wasting away of muscles, and weakness. A low-carbohydrate, high-fat diet is the best prevention.

Ergot: Horny growth found on the back of the fetlock joint

Foal: A baby horse or mule

Founder: A crippling disease of the foot caused by laminitis, the inflammation of the laminae of the foot

Gaited: Mules that move with a four-beat rhythm called a running walk, fox trot, single step, or rack. It is very smooth to ride.

Gelding/gelded: A male mule or horse that has been castrated

Gestation: Period of time from conception to the birth of the foal

Green: Inexperienced; a mule that is in the early stages of training

Hebra: A cross between a female zebra and a male horse

Hinny: An equine hybrid resulting from crossing a male horse with a female donkey

Hybrid: A cross between two different species

Hybrid vigor: The quality of strength in an offspring from two different species. The offspring is stronger than either of its parents.

Immunity: Antibody protection against certain diseases

In-hand class: Classes in a mule or horse show in which the handler leads, rather than rides, the mule or horse

Internal parasites: Organisms that live and feed inside the body of the mule. Round worms, bots, and pinworms are examples of internal parasites.

Jack: A male donkey

Jennet or Jenny: A female donkey

John mule: A castrated male mule

Jack mule: A male mule that has not been castrated and exhibits stallion behaviors, but is sterile

Liberty: Non-ridden movements done by the mule without the use of physical controls such as a halter and lead or bridle

Lipomas: Fatty tumors

Mammoth jack: A donkey that measures fifty-six inches or taller at the withers

Molly mule: A female mule

Mule: An equine hybrid resulting from crossing a male donkey with a female horse

Mule train: A string of pack mules

Mulemen: People who take care of the mules in a mule train

Muleskinner: A person skilled in driving freight wagons pulled by mules, usually a multi-hitch

Navel ill: See shigellosis. Also known as joint ill and sleepy foal disease.

Neonatal isorythrolysis: A disease that destroys the red blood cells in a newborn foal

Novice: An inexperienced mule or horse person

Palfrey: A small mule or horse in the Middle Ages preferred for riding because of its smooth gaits

Parelli Games™: Exercises performed with a horse or mule that were developed by well-known equine clinician Pat Parelli

Parturition: The birth process, including labor and delivery

Placenta: Membranes that connect the fetus to the mare's uterus

Pleasure mule: A mule used for personal recreation and companionship

Quagga: A subspecies of the zebra, now extinct

Ration: The measure of food, hay, or water given per feeding

Roached back: A convex back, common in mules, that makes fitting a traditional saddle difficult

Round pen: A round enclosure in which mules or horses are trained

Scours: Diarrhea in newborn foals

Shigellosis: Septic infection in foals that is usually deadly. Also known as navel ill, joint ill, and sleepy foal disease.

Sire: The father of a mule or horse.

Surrogate mother: A mare that carries a fertilized egg transferred from another mare in her uterus until birth

Telegony: Also known as parental impression; the mistaken theory that if a female is bred to one stallion, then later to another, the offspring of the second stallion can inherit traits from the first stallion.

Testosterone: Male hormone

Thrush: A disease of the foot caused by anaerobic bacteria. Signs are a thick, black discharge and foul odor. Good hygiene and dry environment are the best deterrents.

Umbilical cord: Tissue that attaches the blood vessels from the placenta to the foal

Weaning: Separating the foal from its dam so it can no longer nurse

Weanling: A young foal that has been weaned from its mother and is no longer nursing

Yearling: A foal that is one year old

Zebra mule: A cross between a male horse and a female zebra

Zebrass: A cross between a male zebra and a female donkey

Zebret: A cross between a female zebra and a male donkey

Zebroid: A cross between a zebra and any other equine

Zony: A cross between a pony and a zebra

Zorse: A cross between a horse and a zebra

Bibliography

Books

Attar, Cynthia. *The Mule Companion: A Guide to Understanding the Mule*, 3rd ed. Portland, OR: Partner Communications, 1993.

Ensminger, M. E. *Horses and Horsemanship*, 5th ed. Danville, IL: The Interstate Printers and Publishers, Inc, 1977.

Essin, Emmett M. *Shavetails and Bell Sharps: The History of the U.S. Army Mule*. Lincoln, NE: University of Nebraska Press, 2000.

Evans, J. Warren. *Horses*, 1st ed. San Francisco, CA: W.H. Freeman and Company, 1981.

Hauer, John. *The Natural Superiority of Mules*, 1st ed. Guilford, CT: The Lyons Press, 2005.

Shideler, R. K. and J. L. Voss. *Management of the Pregnant Mare and Newborn Foal*, 1st ed. Fort Collins, CO: Animal Reproduction Laboratory, Colorado State University, 1984.

Stamm, Michael P. *The Mule Alternative: the Saddle Mule in the American West*, 1st ed. Battle Mountain, NV: Medicine Wolf Press, 1992.

Wagoner, Don M. and M. M. Vale, DMV. *The Illustrated Veterinary Encyclopedia for Horsemen*, 2nd ed. Tyler, TX: Equine Research Publications, 1977.

Magazines

Edwards, Steve. "How to Buy a Mule." *Rural Heritage* Autumn 2004: 88-90.

Hunter, Diane. "The Jackass Trail." *Western Mule* May 2007: 22-23.

Pamphlet

Horse Handbook, Housing and Equipment. Fort Collins, CO: Colorado State University Cooperative Extension Service, 1995.

Personal interviews

Amos, Laura, e-mail message to author, 2007

Bartel, Rowdy, e-mail message to author, 2007

Berry, Jennifer, e-mail message to author, 2007

Cox, Deborah, e-mail message to author, 2007

Deschu, Aaron, e-mail message to author, 2008

Finger, Amy, e-mail message to author, 2007

Grace, Jeane, e-mail message to author, 2007

Hoffman, Shannon, e-mail message to author, 2007

King, Sue, e-mail message to author, 2007

Lamm, James, personal interview, 2007

Lemke, Janeen, e-mail message to author, 2007

Lougee, Suzanne, e-mail message to author, 2008

McLeon, Amy, e-mail message to author, 2007

Patton, Leah, e-mail message to author, 2007

Rauh, Vickie, e-mail message to author, 2007

Ross, Cindy, e-mail message to author, 2007

Ryan, Glen, personal interview, 2008

Shannon, Sylvia, e-mail message to author, 2007

Wyatt, Liz, e-mail message to author, 2007

Web sites

"America's Civil War: Horses and Field Artillery." *History Net.* Accessed on April 25, 2007. http://printthis.clickability.com/pt/cpt?action=cpt&title=TheHistory net+%7C=Weap

Baird, Ralph E. "Mars Task Force: a Short History." *Ex-CBI Roundup.* Feb. 1997. Accessed on Sept. 10, 2007. http://cbi-theater-8.home.comcast.net/mars/marstaskforce.html

"Barred M Ranch: Presenting Zebra and Their Hybrids." *Barred-M-Ranch.* Accessed on Aug. 8, 2007. www.nortexinfo.net/BarredMRanch/Zebra.html

Bartels, Rowdy. "Bartels Livestock." *Zebras and Zorses Unlimited.* Accessed on Aug. 30, 2007. www.zebrasandzorsesunlimited.com

Benson Mule Days. Accessed on Oct. 24, 2007. www.bensonmuledays.com

"Bishop Mule Days." *Bishop Mule Days Celebration.* Accessed on Oct. 24, 2007. www.muledays.org

Chandezi, Molly. "Miracle Mule Baby Born in Colorado." Accessed on Nov. 5, 2007. http://winterhawk2.com/hunting/?p=20

Damerow, Gail. "Following the Plow." *Mother Earth News.* Mar.-Apr. 1974. Accessed on Oct. 4, 2007. www.motherearthnews.com/livestock-and-farming/1974-03-01/Following-the-Plow.aspx

————. "Logging the New Fashioned Way." *Mother Earth News.* Apr.-May 1994. Accessed on Sept. 25, 2007. www.motherearthnews.com/livestock-and-farming/1994-04-01/Logging-the-New-Fashioned-Way.aspx

Gill, N. S. "Relative Value of Horses and Mules for Ancient Work." *About.Com.* Accessed on May 28, 2007. http://ancienthistory.about.com/od/dailylife socialcustoms/qt/horseandmule.htm?p=1

Glynn, Karen. "Running Mules: Mule Racing in the Mississippi Delta." *Mississippi Folklife.* University of Mississippi. Accessed on Oct. 13, 2007. www.olemiss.edu/depts/south/publish/missfolk/mfcurris/runmule.html

"Hells Canyon Mule Days." Accessed on Oct. 24, 2007. www.hellscanyonmule days.com

Rolling over . . .

Hixon, Celia. "The Marvelous Mule." Accessed on April 19, 2007. www .eclectica.org/v1n2/hixon.html

Hutchins, Betsy. "24 Points to Consider When Mule Shopping." *Rural Heritage*. Sept. 15, 2000. Accessed on April 22, 2007. www.ruralheritage.com/mule_paddock/ mule_buy2.htm

Hutchins, Paul, and Betsy Hutchins. "Why Mules?" *Rural Heritage*. Accessed on Aug. 30, 2007. www.ruralheritage.com/mule_paddock/mule_why.htm

"Hybrids & Mutants Index." *Messy Beast*. Accessed on Aug. 1, 2007. www.messy beast.com/genetics/hybrids-equines.htm

Ingersoll, Ernest. "Rocky Mountain Mules." *Cornell University Library*. Accessed on April 25, 2007. http://cdl.library.cornell.edu/cgi-bin/moa/moa-cig? notisid=ABP7664-0019-152

Josephus. "The Roman Army in the First Century CE." *Ancient History Source- book: Josephus (37-After 93CE)*. Accessed on May 28, 2007. http://forham .edu/Halsall/ancient/josephus-warb.html

Kuchta, David. "Mine Mules." *The No. 9 Mine & Museum Lansford, PA*. Accessed on July 26, 2007. http://no9mine.tripod.com/id11.html

Lindelof, Bill. "Sierra Gold Mine Wants to Return to Mule Power." *California Gold Rush*. Accessed on Sept. 4, 2007. www.calgoldrush.com/extra/mules.html

Long, E. B. "Transportation and Commerce in the Civil War." *Civil War*. Oct. 25, 2004. Accessed on Sept. 30, 2007. www.civilwarhome.com/transcom.htm

Macgill, Ruth. "How the Mail Went Through—Colonial Times, the Jackass Mail, Pony Express and Butterfield." Accessed on Oct. 8, 2007. www.gather.com/view/ ArticlePF.jsp?articleeId=281474976998722

Malcher, Marlene. "To Make a Mule." *Rural Heritage*. Accessed on Sept. 4, 2007. www
.ruralheritage.com/mule_paddock/mule_breeding.htm

"Management Recommendations for Donkeys and Mules." *Ontario Ministry of
Agriculture, Food and Rural Affairs*. Accessed on Oct. 29, 2007. http://www
.omafra.gov.on.ca/english/livestock/horses/facts/info_mules.htm

McCarty, Jim. "The Long-eared Loggers." *Rural Missouri*. Accessed on Jan. 2008.
http://www.ruralmissouri.org/08JanMuleLoggers.html

McLean, Amy K., Dr. Mel Yokoyama, and Dr. Sue Hengemuehle. "Donkeys and Mule
Scenarios: When to Stop, Think, Read or Call." Accessed on Oct. 19, 2007.
www.maulesel.info/my_favorite_mule_is_a_hinny.html

Morris, Sarah. "Midas as Mule: Anatolia in Greek Myth and Phrygian Kingship."
American Philological Association. Jan. 2004. Accessed on July 11, 2007. www
.apaclassics.org/AnnualMeeting/04mtg/abstracts/MORRIS.html

"The Mule as a Cultural Invention." *Santa Clarita Valley History in Pictures*. 1990.
U.S. Borax, Inc. Accessed on July 24, 2007. www.scvhistory.com/scvhis
tory/borax-20muleteam.htm

"Mule Day, Calvary, Georgia." Accessed on Oct. 24, 2007. www.caironet.com/MULE.
htm

"Mule Day 2007." *Mules and Maury County 1807-2007*. Accessed on Oct. 24, 2007.
www.muleday.com

Patton, Leah. "Healthy as a Horse, Stubborn as a Mule." *Saddle Mule News*.
Accessed on Oct. 7, 2007. www.saddlemulenews.com/healthy_as_a_horse
.htm

Pearce, Basil C. "The Jackass Mail San Antonio and San Diego Mail Line." *San
Diego Historical Society*. Accessed on Oct. 8, 2007. www.sandiegohistory
.org/journal/69spring/jackass.htm

"The Ranch." *Spots N Stripes Ranch*. Accessed on Aug. 9, 2007. www.spots
nstripes.com/aboutus.htm

Rees, James C. "George Washington: A Truly Remarkable Man." *Masonic World*. Feb.
1991. Accessed on May 6, 2006. www.masonicworld.com/education/files/
mar03/george_washington.htm

Rees, Simon. "Featured Articles: the Forgotten War." *First World War*. June 19,
2004. Accessed on Sept. 30, 2007. www.firstworldwar.com/features/
forgottenarmy.htm

"Restoring the Quagga." *Nature*. Accessed on Aug. 2, 2007. www.pbs.org/wnet/
nature/horsetigers/quagga.html

Roberts, Cindy K. "Mule Feet—What Your Farrier Should Know." *Every Cow Girl's
Dream*. Accessed on Aug. 30, 2007. www,everycowgirlsdream.com/mulefeet.
html

Schlosser, S. E. "The Greenhorn and the Mule Egg." *American Folktales*. Accessed on
Oct. 10, 2007. www.americanfolklore.net/folktales/ks3.html

... and over ...

"Stable, Mule Shed and Paddock." *Mount Vernon.* Accessed on April 25, 2007. www.mountvernon.org/visit/plan/index.cfm/pid/284

"Telegony." *Wikipedia.* Accessed on Aug. 8, 2007. http://en.wikipedia.org/wiki/Telegony_%28pregnancy%29

Thrapp, Qmc, 1st Lt. Don L. "The Mules of Mars." *Army Quarter Master Museum—Fort Lee, Virginia.* May 28, 2001. Army Quartermaster Corp Web. Accessed on 2 Oct. 2007. www.qmmuseum.lee.army.mil/WWII/mules_of_mars.htm

Valentine, Beth A., Dvm, Phd. "EPSM—Muscle Disease in Draft Horses." *Rural Heritage.* Accessed on Aug. 30, 2007. www.ruralheritage.com/vet_clinic.epsm.htm

Vargo, Cecile P. "Ghostly White Mule Tales From the Mines of Bodie." *Explore Historic California.* Accessed on Oct. 10, 2007. http://explorehistoriccalif.com/oct06.html

"What is a Mule Made of?" *Pet Columns.* April 20, 1998. University of Illinois College of Veterinary Medicine. Accessed on Oct. 5, 2007. www.cvm.uiuc.edu/petcolumns/showarticle.cfm?id=123

Index

Italicized page references indicate illustrations.

... and over.

About the Author

Donna Campbell Smith is a freelance writer who has contributed to several magazines, including *Western Mule Magazine, Stable Management Magazine, The Gaited Horse, USA Equestrian, Young Rider, Boys Life, The Chronicle of the Horse, Conquistador, Our State,* and *Carolina Country.*

She has worked in the horse industry for more than thirty years. She is the author of *The Book of Miniature Horses* and *The Book of Draft Horses.* Donna has a degree in equine technology, has served more than twenty years in the NC 4-H Horse Program, and is a certified riding instructor.

She lives in Franklinton, North Carolina.